HOW TO REDUCE YOUR PATIENTS' CHRONIC PAIN:

A NEW MODEL TO RESTORE HOPE

(Theirs and Yours!)

Dr. George Beilin
Licensed Psychologist

Peter —
I'm sure you'll find this book
helpful!
Look forward to [illegible] [illegible]
[illegible] [illegible]
[illegible]

Copyright and Publishing Information

ISBN 978-0-9996198-3-4
E-book 978-0-9996198-4-1
First edition: 2018

Editor: Kate Victory Hannisian, Blue Pencil Consulting
Book and Cover Design: Brian Murphy Art and Design
Printing: King Printing Co., Inc.

This book is
dedicated to the thousands of
health practitioners who
treat individuals with
chronic pain daily.

Helping your patients take the first step out of
the swamp is the hardest.

Contents

Foreword

Thank goodness, the urgent need for a truthsayer has been answered in this wonderfully thoughtful book by Dr. George Beilin. As a dedicated health-care professional, you will benefit from reading the book's ample wisdom, a powerful salve with the potential to help your patients experience enriched living.

Chronic pain is not only an increasingly pervasive medical condition, as Dr. Beilin explains, but also one that is uniquely challenging for you and your colleagues. Your patients' pain can be intractable with persistent, continuous or intermittent debilitating symptoms. It's hard to define and to target with effective, economical and safe treatments. Chronic pain is exceedingly complex because it is so multifaceted and not entirely predictable. Ambiguous working definitions and the limitations of language and speech to express and communicate the human experience of pain complicate the situation. Relying exclusively on drug-based interventions can create dependencies on substances like opioids, which can become addictive and even lethal. We see a crisis because that trend has reached epidemic proportions. There's a real need for a safer way to manage chronic pain.

We humans are sensitive creatures who pride ourselves on being intelligent life forms. Yet pain touches the deepest and most fundamental spiritual, philosophical and religious ways of understanding that bind our families and societies together in pursuit of progress. Because these conditions and societies are not entirely consistent or sometimes even compatible, their notions of human behavior and motivation are sometimes hard to reconcile. No wonder healers can seem so inconsistent to patients in dire need of immediate answers. That same obstacle is exasperating and frustrates the very self-confidence and motivation that your patients need in order to sustain their recovery efforts. The disappointments and delays also trigger reactions that deplete the perseverance and good intentions of supporting your patients' families and friends, and Dr. Beilin teaches us that this can also interfere with progress or even set back the best efforts of all involved.

Indeed, chronic pain is a quagmire with contradictions and competing agendas and priorities at every turn. For Heaven's sake, what can your patients do to avoid hopeless despair, frivolous expenditures of energy and precious finances, and instead actually produce genuine healing and resolution?

Fortunately, Dr. George Beilin contributes something that is comprehensive in its scope, heartfelt, readily understandable, and remarkably likely to be effective. In my long career as a healthcare provider and an attorney, I have experienced many people with serious medical and physical conditions, as well as emotional and psychological ones. These people experience excruciating distress both from the pain and the stressors of modern life. I have been working for many decades in teaching hospitals (such as Massachusetts General Hospital/Harvard Medical School and Tufts Medical School), public agencies and state facilities, the military and at Harvard Law School. As a clinician, teacher and supervisor, I can certainly attest that my colleague Dr. Beilin is one of the most outstanding and brilliant professionals I have encountered, and he well deserves my highest respect and regard for his understanding, compassion, expertise, skill, ethics and empathetic concern. It is my pleasure to encourage you to read carefully and follow the sound advice he has laid out so elegantly and sensibly in this book.

Dr. Beilin has drawn upon and blended resources from Western and Eastern cultural traditions in order to create a comprehensive coping stratagem to help you understand your patients' most compelling life challenges, including chronic pain.

What I appreciate most is his offering of methodical exercises and approaches your patients can use to improve their life experiences in the face of many different challenges, especially those they face in having chronic pain. Dr. Beilin's new model does a superior job of distinguishing adaptive from maladaptive strategies for pain management and boosting motivation necessary to achieve, sustain and renew the motivation that's essential for change. His model is also based on standard empirical assessment and monitoring procedures to more reliably detect, measure and document actual experiential results.

What I find most impressive in George's model is his incorporation of the most recent and powerful understanding in the field of psychology regarding choice and free will. The eminent Israeli psychologist Daniel Kahneman, author of *Thinking, Fast and Slow*, won a Nobel Prize for the groundbreaking research that he and my graduate school classmate Amos Tversky conducted in behavioral economics theory. They studied how people really make choices, considering that humans are not entirely rational, but instead subject to profound cognitive biases and heuristic thinking. In his book, Dr. Beilin superbly explains in professional terms this remarkably important refinement of Freudian notions about dynamic unconscious that have prevailed for the past century. The genius in these insights is that cognitive appraisal becomes a tool that your chronic pain patients can use to reduce the panoply of their types of "pain." Dr. Beilin correctly explains that your patients' painful experiences are really not simply medical phenomena but are instead an amalgam of physical, emotional, life stressors and other factors.

Dr. George Beilin's insights are truly the fruition and culmination of both the Western cultural tradition's pathways for understanding human nature and the Eastern tradition's contributions of meditational mindfulness. "Positive psychology," à la Dr. Martin Seligman, a former president of the American Psychological Association, is a cornerstone of Dr. Beilin's methodology, which has distilled and translated the pivotal aspects of time-honored and tested wisdom for coping. Dr. Beilin's book brings contemporary insights about human nature and societal organization to key ideas from the third century BC in a form that reflects the Age of Reason and modern science.

Best wishes on your journey using Dr. Beilin's model for helping your patients attain a Pain Management Lifestyle. They have suffered enough and no longer need to be saddled with the disabling and debilitating pain that has been torturing them. It is time for you to help them take control and seize their opportunity to live fully and unencumbered by misery.

Steven Nisenbaum, PhD, JD
Medical Staff, Psychiatry Department,
Massachusetts General Hospital/School of Medicine
Assistant Clinical Professor in Public Health and Community Medicine,
Tufts Medical School

Let's welcome Chronic Pain! Right here! On our stage!

Introduction

You wake up early, ready to start your day at the office, knowing full well that your healthcare practice has changed dramatically over time. You are already stressing out, thinking about having to see a multitude of patients, each of whom has differing complaints, symptoms and histories that you have to review, then record in a detailed, cumbersome electronic heath record (EHR) you are now required to use. You feel frustrated, knowing full well that you will, most likely, spend little time with each patient because of your large caseload and the note-taking and administrative demands placed on you.

You get to your office and begin your first encounter by greeting your patient, then reviewing their record and medication list. You refine it if any medications or medication amounts have changed as indicated in the patient's EHR. Next, you ask for and record their present symptoms. As you listen to the patient share their concerns, you type away on your laptop. You know you don't want to fall behind with seeing patients and note-taking because it will only mean that you'll be going home later than usual, or you'll have to catch up on recording notes later or the next day.

Suddenly, you become irritable, recognizing that the symptoms your patient is describing are similar to those described during their previous visits. Typically, these are complaints of experiencing chronic physical pain, complaints that you surmise may have had no clear, physical evidence to support them. You realize that it isn't going to be so easy for you to recommend anything new. You've advised so many options before with which the patient rarely improved or complied. Nothing is working.

If you are a physician or clinical nurse practitioner, you may have prescribed medications like NSAIDS, muscle relaxants, or opiates. You may have performed certain procedures, or advised patients to engage in healthy activities like simple stretching, exercising, or cutting down their weight or alcohol intake. You may have authorized or reviewed their X-rays, blood tests or MRIs to try to substantiate the rationale for their physical complaints. A majority of the medical tests seemed useless because the patient still complained of having chronic pain. You've even made periodic referrals to specialists, like orthopedic surgeons, physical therapists, or chiropractors, despite knowing the patient's level of treatment adherence was minimal. You wonder if your patient is looking for a quick fix of an opioid medication you once prescribed so easily, but can't anymore, because of federal and state regulations that restrict them. You even wonder if they're looking for a marijuana card. Or, you begin to mistrust them, wondering if they're looking for a disability diagnosis, a process that will require more of your precious, limited time to procure documentation and complete detailed forms. You feel more frustrated and helpless! No matter what advice you give them, nothing seems to work.

After talking to and examining your patient, it seems obvious to you that their pain persists. There is no perfect answer you can give them to rid themselves completely of their pain. You feel so helpless that you may recommend that they go to a pain management center because you're clear there's nothing more you can do for them.

If you are a physical, occupational or rehabilitation therapist, a chiropractor, a mental health clinician, or even an acupuncturist, masseuse, or any other healthcare provider, you may believe that you have done your best to help your chronic pain patients improve and feel less pained. You hope that they can improve with your help. Like your medical colleagues, you can become discouraged and frustrated, feeling helpless because, despite all the listening, empathy and ongoing support (physical or emotional) you provide your patients, it doesn't change their complaints.

Does this sound familiar? If so, then you are not alone! The number of patients reporting physical symptoms of chronic pain, or pain that lasts longer than three to six months, is increasing exponentially each year. A 2011 report by the Institute of Medicine of the National Academies (now the National Academy of Medicine) indicated that approximately 100 million individuals in the United States complain of having chronic, physical pain. A report from Global Industry Analysts, Inc. in that same year declared that the number is 1.5 billion people worldwide or 3% to 4.5% of the global population. An NIH study published in the *Journal of Pain* (March 2015) noted that "126.1 million adults reported some pain in the previous 3 months with 25.3 million adults (11.2%) suffering from daily (chronic) pain and 23.4 million (10.3%) reporting a lot of pain." According to an article in *Practice Fusion* (June 2016), back pain has become one of the ten highest ICD-10 diagnoses of major medical conditions for which patients seek treatment. An overview of American pain surveys by the National Fibromyalgia and Chronic Pain Association in 2015 reported that 4 out of 10 people with chronic pain say it impacts their overall quality of life. Seventy-seven percent of patients with chronic pain further report feeling depressed, while 86% report they don't sleep well (American Academy of Pain Association, 2016).

The 2011 Institute of National Academies report further noted that it costs the United States between $560 and $635 billion dollars annually, some $261 to $300 billion of which is due to incremental costs in health care and $297-$336 billion of which is due to lost productivity.

The most serious condition is the exponential increase in drug overdoses from prescription opioid medications and from street drugs like heroin mixed with toxic fentanyl. The Centers for Disease Control reports that "opioids (including prescription opioids, heroin, and fentanyl) killed more than 42,000 people in 2016, more than any year on record. Forty percent of all opioid overdose deaths involve a prescription opioid." *Bloomberg News* reported that the drug Oxycontin generated $1.8 billion in sales in 2017 for its maker, Purdue Pharma, LP.

Despite the major focus on opiates by the federal and state governments, opiate usage is just one serious problem facing Americans and people worldwide. A study reported in *Clinical Psychiatry News* (February 2018) noted that, "Of the 14,834 suicide deaths from 18 states in 2014, tests for alcohol -- conducted for 53% (7,883) of decedents -- were the most commonly performed and were the second most likely to be positive among drugs with data available. The rate was 40.2%." (Seventy percent of the positive results had blood alcohol concentrations of .08 g/dL or higher.) "Antidepressants had the highest positivity rate for drugs included in the analysis: 40.8% of 3,682 tests conducted in 2014." Benzodiazepines were identified as the next most commonly seen drug (32.6%), followed by opiates (30%) and marijuana (21%). There seemed to be a higher correlation between the use of antidepressants and alcohol than between any other substances.

More patients appear to be living a "passive suicide" lifestyle as a way to cope with having chronic pain. Many of them are overweight, prone to diabetes or cardiovascular conditions, get little to no exercise, and continue to drink excessive amounts of alcohol and/or smoke tobacco daily. The *New York Times* (March 2018) revealed that nearly 40% of Americans were obese in 2015 and 2016. An NIH study (June 2015) found that alcohol use disorders (AUDs) were on the increase over the past decade. "Nearly one-third of adults in the United States have an AUD at some time in their lives, but only 20% seek treatment. Even overdose deaths from cocaine use have doubled since 2010 to 2015." (NIDA, September 2017)

As a licensed professional who has worked in the mental health field for over 46 years, I have become deeply concerned about what is happening to you, the healthcare provider, given your level of stress from all the changes in the healthcare system, the need to keep up with the frenetic pace of seeing your patients daily, and your requirement to document copious electronic health record notes. I hear many of your colleagues' concerns almost daily, listening to them commiserate during lunch hour about the extent of stress they are undergoing. Their concerns underscore the seriousness of information provided at a local seminar by a chief psychiatrist who represented the Physicians Health Services, Inc., a corporation of the Massachusetts Medical Society that specializes in helping physicians who are experiencing burnout. He acknowledged that their service caseload had increased dramatically in 2017, with more than 400 physicians and medical students being helped for mental health and substance abuse problems. One in three professionals were self-referred because of occupational stress, difficulties balancing work and family, and difficulty dealing with stress and financial pressures. Many of them are on active monitoring contracts for substance abuse.

I believe that one of the main reasons many professionals in the healthcare community are overstressed is because they place unrealistic expectations on themselves to help so many patients change their behaviors, especially when it comes to more difficult conditions like chronic pain. These professionals want to see their patients improve, if not conquer, their pain, because that's what they were trained to do. And this includes you! As a healthcare provider, your positive desire to find the right treatment or cure for pain patients may not be so easy to realize. Why? Because the definition of chronic pain and the treatment expectations and strategies are changing dramatically, as you'll read in this book.

My hope is that, as any type of healthcare provider who works with patients having chronic pain, you will find the information in the coming chapters helpful enough that you can become less stressed. By changing your perspective about the paradigm of "pain" as being much more than simply physical symptoms, I hope that you can reduce your own high self-standards, and the expectations of your patients to change, and that you realize you are "good enough" in doing everything possible to help your patients.

Treating chronic pain requires an ongoing team effort, of which you are an integral member. Having the support of other healthcare providers as extended team members can help you reduce your own stress, given the multidimensional and subjective nature of chronic pain and the fact that treating chronic pain implies simply trying to reduce it over time, in a manner similar to many other bio-psycho-social medical conditions.

Because it needed to be done!

Chapter 1: Why I Wrote This Book

You may be asking, "Who is this psychologist who is writing such a book on chronic pain, especially for me, a healthcare provider who specializes in this area? What gives him the legitimate authority to write on this topic?"

Those are excellent questions and I'm glad that you're asking them. They are definitely ones I had thought about much, especially before writing my first book, *How to Reduce Your Chronic Pain: A New Model to Help You Restore Hope*, a book that speaks directly to your patients and their caretakers. If you haven't read or skimmed through my first book, I'll start with an overview of my professional and personal reasons for writing this sequel for you and the other healthcare professionals who specialize in pain management.

My Educational Years

From September 1968 to December 1969, I attended Ohio State University in Columbus, Ohio, then transferred to New York University, where I obtained my bachelor's degree in psychology in the summer of 1972. Washington Square, in the heart of New York City's Greenwich Village, had been, and still is, a major center of creativity for music, art, theater and dance. When I was there, we had to attend most classes in nearby brownstones surrounding the main buildings because there was a bomb scare almost daily connected to the protests over the war in Vietnam. People in our country were experiencing much life stressor pain, intermixed with much emotional pain of anger and sadness, although many Americans still felt proud that our country was engaged in such an allegedly "moral" war. The same held true for our brethren who served and fought in Vietnam, although many experienced trauma from fear of guerilla warfare and the use of such chemicals as Agent Orange but tried to dull their angst by self-medicating using substances. Many American tried to overcome their pain by remaining resilient through the creative expression of songs, poetry, paintings, and other artistic modalities. Others asserted themselves by participating in marches and peace rallies and by becoming activists.

When the pain of the Vietnam War was beginning to die down, I entered graduate school in psychology at Boston University. Here, I obtained my master's degree in 1974 and my doctoral degree in 1976. During this time, I completed multiple clinical internships, including a field placement at the Tufts University Inpatient Psychiatry Unit at Boston State Hospital in the Mattapan neighborhood of Boston, Massachusetts. I then did a clinical internship at a community mental health center (CMHC) in Lawrence, Massachusetts, and another paid internship at a CMHC in Lynn, Massachusetts.

The patients I saw in treatment at Boston State Hospital (and others discussed by staff and interns in team meetings and in case presentations by a staff psychiatrist) had severe mental illness. They were diagnosed with various forms of schizophrenia or manic depression (later to be termed bipolar disorder). Many suffered from post-traumatic stress disorder (PTSD) emanating from painful years of abuse or neglect.

While on the unit, I observed, and learned much about, the pain and intense suffering of these patients. Many of them had been on the unit for years and were prescribed major tranquilizers like Stelazine, Thorazine or Haldol, or mood stabilizers like lithium carbonate or Depakote. These medicines helped patients stay calm by allowing them to retreat from an outer world of pain from mistrust, deprivation or trauma, into an inner world of escapist delusions, hallucinations, and interpersonal isolation that provided them with greater comfort, even if it meant they lived in a locked facility replete with dark, quiet-cornered spaces, echoing screams and limited nutrition. Some patients were administered electro-convulsive therapy (ECT) and many sought intermittent placements in isolation rooms when their inner world of comfort from pain was suddenly breached by interludes of attempted human interactions or of overwhelming, traumatic memories.

At the Lawrence CMHC, I learned much about the different levels of pain of patients who reached healthier developmental milestones than those patients at Boston State Hospital, but who still experienced cognitive and emotional pain from life stressors, like major losses, or from a lack of fortitude or ego strength. Many had poor frustration tolerance while others had difficulties in delaying gratification or had interpersonal deficits from deprived or abusive parenting or from poor socialization. Many patients suffered from the pain of severe anxiety and/or depression that emanated from irrational cognitive appraisals of negative thoughts and emotional pain from fears, or from excessive guilt or pain from losses and from feeling hopeless and helpless. Other patients assigned to me, or discussed at team meetings, had tried to commit suicide or had experienced much pain from frequent panic attacks or suffered from PTSD, since they had been victims of severe abuse or neglect from birth. Other patients internalized their cognitive, emotional and interpersonal pain by developing various psychosomatic conditions, while some self-medicated to avoid their cognitive and emotional pain by abusing drugs or alcohol.

Although I was trained in a traditional psychoanalytic model, I still learned specific skills critical for most therapeutic approaches, including the ability to listen, empathize, support and interpret the relationship between how patients coped in adaptive or maladaptive ways with various sorts of cognitive, emotional, interpersonal and physical pain.

The same held true during my clinical internship at the Lynn CMHC, where I saw many patients with similar painful conditions. During this time, and even through the 1980s and '90s, I learned to use different therapeutic modalities; in particular, those of prominent family therapists like Salvador Minuchin, Murray Bowen, Carl Whitaker and James Haley, who wrote about different systems' approaches to treating patients within their family context. These family-system models were invaluable and quite effective, especially when trying to make therapeutic changes for patients in pain within short-term, goal-oriented treatment. One example was my learning how a patient's physical symptoms could have so much power and influence to control other family members or to be able to turn the focus away from other family conflicts, like marital discord or abuse or masked substance dependence. Murray Bowen even identified how dysfunctional family patterns could be repeated over multiple generations.

How did your professional training help you appreciate
how physical pain can emanate from multiple sources, like life
stressors of trauma, losses, or family or interpersonal conflicts,
or from intense emotional states, or difficulties in negative
thinking or a lack of fortitude?

What judgments have you made about what causes
chronic pain, given its bio-psycho-social aspects?

My Professional Years

Following my graduation in May 1976, I obtained my first full-time paid position as the clinical director of a regional inpatient adolescent unit at Danvers State Hospital, Danvers, Massachusetts. Our task as a clinical team was to reduce the inpatient adolescent census by taking teenagers who were locked in different units out of them and placing them in a day treatment program replete with educational and therapeutic treatment, including individual, group, family and expressive therapies. Periodically, we had to restrain those teenagers who expressed their intense pain by becoming violent or by cutting themselves. Medications helped to regulate these self-destructive behaviors, but I believe it was their being in a milieu of constant caring, support and understanding that bettered their pain. Eventually, we reduced the state hospital adolescent census from about fifty to about seven, sending patients into various community placements aligned with the philosophy of de-institutionalization, implemented by then-Governor of Massachusetts Michael Dukakis.

After becoming the administrative director of the so-called "Solstice" program, I found a residential site in Rowley, Massachusetts, to move the program out of the state hospital and into the community, where it belonged. Eventually, Solstice became a state model of a successful residential therapeutic-educational milieu for adolescents who suffered from severe mental illness.

Just prior to the move, I decided to take a temporary position as the associate area director of the regional Lynn-area office for the Commonwealth of Massachusetts Department of Mental Health (DMH), but I finally found my niche as a full-time outpatient psychologist in private practice in Beverly, Massachusetts. I have remained there to this day, first starting out by collaborating with two colleagues with whom I shared a small downtown Beverly office space. I then established an incorporated practice called The Beverly Center, PC., a group of interdisciplinary clinicians who collaborated to provide psychiatric and psychological services, including medication management, neuro-psychological testing, and psychotherapy in an office building I purchased in 1983.

During my time as both an administrator and clinician of the Beverly Center, I learned valuable lessons about running a mental health group practice by remaining cognitively flexible to adapt to the system's quick-changing healthcare environment, no different than what you experience today. Insurance company personnel demanded an extensive rationale for any behavioral health authorizations and re-authorizations as a way to try to reduce expenditures, then micro-managed the sessions by requiring an array of different assessment forms that changed rapidly over time. As mental health professionals, we had to be credentialed, then re-credentialed by each insurance company, every two to three years. Many insurance companies' explanation of benefits (EOBs) had many mistakes that took a large chunk of non-reimbursable time to fix. The "pain" from systems stress seemed endless, given the perceived contradictory priorities between providing quality mental healthcare and keeping up with insurance company demands and changes. We always seemed to be catching up with their changing practice requirements and ways to avoid malpractice litigation. New federal privacy (HIPPA) laws demanded even more in the way of continued risk-management training and giving patients a multitude of legal forms to complete before attending their first few treatment sessions.

How have the changing healthcare demands impacted the level of "professional pain" you experience in trying to practice offensive, rather than defensive, medicine?

I managed to sustain my love for the profession despite the onslaught of these forever-changing administrative policies and reimbursement conflicts. Most importantly, I learned to perceive each patient's pain in a unique way. This implied that no matter how simplified the physical diagnosis needed to be for insurance billing purposes, each patient I saw had a different genetic predisposition, temperament, developmental history of strengths and limitations, interpersonal relationship style, life stressors and different physical, cognitive, and emotional ways to express their pain, especially pain from a lack of fortitude or ego strength. Not one patient was the same. Variety became the spice of life. In graduate school, I learned to call this the phenomenological approach to treating each patient.

I further learned to apply a particular theoretical approach, namely, the trans-theoretical model of motivational change, developed and researched by James O. Prochaska and Carlo DiClemente in the 1980s. The authors theorized that patients are at different stages of change, ranging from a pre-contemplative or denial stage, to a contemplative or ambivalent stage, to a determination or commitment stage, to an action stage, then a maintenance stage whereby a patient's commitment to changing their behavior occurred over time. As any type of healthcare provider, you must know where a patient is, in their intrinsic desire to change their behaviors, even if they have regressed at some point to an earlier stage of change. For example, I learned that you can't give advice to a patient if he denies having a problem, or if he isn't sure about wanting to change his behaviors, even if they are maladaptive. Giving advice when a patient isn't ready to change will only lead to treatment non-adherence.

What beliefs do you have about the way to measure successful treatment when you diagnose and treat a patient who complains of having chronic pain? What do you think, and how do you feel, when you make specific treatment recommendations, then find that your patient may show minimal treatment adherence to your recommendations over time?

I further aligned with the relapse prevention model for substance dependence, as theorized by G. A. Marlatt, who suggested that factors like knowing high-risk situations, having effective coping skills, and knowing one's urges and cravings, all contribute to a patient's ability to avoid relapse over time. Specific interventions to reduce the number of relapses include the following:

1. Identifying specific high-risk situations
2. Enhancing the patient's skills for coping with those situations
3. Increasing the patient's level of self-efficacy
4. Modifying the patient's cognitive beliefs about substance effects
5. Managing lapses
6. Restructuring the client's perceptions of the relapse process.

Marlatt's relapse prevention model aligned beautifully with Prochaska and DiClemente's maintenance stage of change. In essence, a patient who becomes committed to changing their behaviors first has to lose or reduce previous behaviors, then maintain new behaviors towards their symptoms over time. This is true for any medical condition, like a person's level of alcohol or tobacco consumption, diabetes, excess weight, and chronic pain.

I continued to practice in Beverly, Massachusetts, and eventually became affiliated with local area hospitals by gaining allied health courtesy privileges and various advanced degrees, including one in administration and management from Harvard University's Extension School, and an American Psychological Association certification as a specialist in substance use and abuse.

In 2008, following my personal experiences with chronic pain (which I will share with you soon), I began to focus more on treating patients with chronic pain. After reading extensively and taking many seminars on pain, I became the chief psychologist for the Pain Management Center at the Lahey Outpatient Center in Danvers, Massachusetts, where I assessed and treated patients who, according to the anesthesiologists and clinical nurse practitioners working there, needed psychological help for co-morbid depression, anxiety, or a dual diagnosis of substance dependence. Many patients referred to me had much anger and poor frustration tolerance about having chronic pain. Many wanted the immediate gratification of pain elimination through medications like opioids, rather than consider other ways to deal with their chronic pain. Many of these patients experienced pain from major life stressors like marital and family conflicts, employment disruptions and financial burdens. Many developed negative cognitive distortions and beliefs about themselves, their relationships with others, and their future. Of most concern were those patients who had severe difficulties with a lack of fortitude. They had problems coping, and had low self-esteem, a lack of resilience, or lowered optimism. Many had poor executive functioning, manifesting as deficits in problem-solving, self-monitoring and cognitive flexibility. Their use of humor seemed limited, if not extinguished, as did any feelings of happiness, gratitude or love, either for themselves or for another person. Faith in G-d or a higher power was minimal, if nonexistent.

In addition to providing much-needed individual therapy to the patient or therapy with the patient's caretaker or family, I chose to initiate and lead a free, weekly chronic pain support group for almost seven years. The group was open to any patient having chronic pain and to their caretakers (spouses or significant friends). This group became an invaluable resource in an area of Massachusetts where very few, if any, similar support groups existed.

Initially, the group structure was to simply allow patients to share their war stories, especially about being angry at the medical community for alleged misdiagnoses, alleged failed medical procedures or the withholding of "quick-fix" medical prescriptions. Patients in the group supported one another by empathizing and by offering helpful suggestions for coping.

At some point during the first year, it became clear that greater structure was needed for these sessions, even if it meant including a short period of mindfulness meditation or a stress management activity. Such activities included listening to calm music or to a relaxation tape that focused on diaphragmatic breathing, progressive muscle relaxation, visual imagery or body scanning, as recommended and utilized by Jon Kabat-Zinn at the University of Massachusetts Medical Center pain clinic. (He had written a book on his experiences, entitled *Full Catastrophe Living.*)

During the second year, I provided even more structure to the hour-and-a-half group sessions. This consisted of an initial ten-minute period of mindfulness meditation, then some educational discussion about a chronic pain topic, then a guest speaker who shared professional expertise or personal experiences in working with chronic pain patients. Typically, this was someone in the medical field who specialized in treating chronic pain patients or patients who had chronic pain and demonstrated incredible resilience. Afterwards, I invited patients to share some jokes about having pain or about the medical profession. The use of humor helped patients reduce the irrationality of thinking that pain was always "painful." The group session ended with time for willing patients to share a personal concern and ask for help from other group members in problem-solving or simply learning to cope.

After almost seven years of facilitating this open-ended weekly group that included anywhere from three to twelve members, I decided that the best way to help more of the millions of people suffering from chronic pain was to write a book. I conceptualized a model for dealing with chronic pain that I had tried and tested over time. It included the element of free choice to defend against or acknowledge unhealthy ways to deal with pain and included a critical need to determine how motivated each patient was to change their behavior. If they could let go or mourn the way they were before having chronic pain, they would have a much better chance of choosing an ongoing "pain management lifestyle" that differed for each person.

The requirement that a patient self-monitor their progress over time became extremely critical, so I created and used some additional pain-rating scales to help each person assess subjectively how they experienced chronic pain. While I found the standard, subjective rating scale (rating one's level of physical pain on a scale of 1 to 10) to be extremely helpful, it didn't take into account the multidimensional aspects of perceiving pain. It was clear to me that each patient had to use additional pain scales to rate and self-monitor life stressors, emotional states, errors in thinking, and lack of fortitude.

I adhered to the theoretical assumption that chronic pain had to be reframed as a metaphor for both good and bad experiences of multidimensional aspects of pain, and that pain, as we redefined it, would be ongoing and never eliminated, but could be lowered or raised by choosing, testing out, then using continuously (or modifying) specific therapeutic options from an array of pain management techniques. It was clear that a patient's belief that they could rely on a quick fix to end their chronic pain was a myth, as was any healthcare provider's belief that someone could eliminate chronic pain once and for all by utilizing just one strategy, such as being prescribed medication, like an opiate.

How Developing Chronic Pain Changed My Professional Life

My personal experiences in developing chronic pain were sequential, starting first with my being, like many people, someone who loved athletics and exercised regularly and vigorously throughout my early and middle years. (A thorough review of my experiences with chronic pain is included in my first book, *How to Reduce Your Chronic Pain: A New Model to Help You Restore Hope*, 2018).

I played a lot of tennis, jogged, ran three Boston Marathons, hiked, skied, and biked, but then developed peripheral neuropathy around 2007. At this point, I had to grieve, or mourn, playing tennis and jogging. Letting go of tennis was especially hard for me since I grew up in a family that loved racket sports. I was very good at it, but my parents didn't have the finances for me to take ongoing tennis lessons or play in local or regional tournaments. As well, I had a father who was a handball champion of the Bronx, in New York City. My parents even met and fell in love on a handball court at Orchard Beach, in Pelham Bay Park in the Bronx.

While continuing to engage in alternative exercise, I experienced a traumatic event in August 2008 that eventually led to my needing an emergency cervical laminectomy in December of that same year. This was followed by a need for a spinal fusion with instrumentation at L4-L5 due to my having severe spinal stenosis, then two partial hemilaminotomies and two hip replacements, all in a span of seven years that ended in February 2016. Like many other aging Americans, I became a full-fledged "bionic person."

Now that I have shared with you my professional and personal experiences in treating and having chronic pain, let's move on to a review of the importance of identifying yourself as being on, or an extension of, your patients' Pain Management Team.

Choosing A
"Pain Management Lifestyle"

Either By

ACKNOWLEDGING IT OR
DEFENDING AGAINST IT

FREE CHOICE!

... in this corner, "The Dream Team."

Chapter 2: The Pain Management Team

Typically, the pain management team usually consists of the patient's primary care physician, clinical nurse practitioner, physician or medical assistant and a licensed clinician trained to help patients work through the sequence of stages in the Pain Management Lifestyle model as discussed in Chapter 4.

The primary care physician is most responsible for serving as the team captain who communicates and coordinates with other specialists to make sure patients are being followed responsibly to help them lower their chronic pain over time. That's a large task for a medical professional who has limited time, given the number of patients they see daily, the demands for posting all encounters in electronic health records, including authorizations for certain tests (like X-rays and blood work), authorizations to see certain healthcare specialists, and authorizations for medications and prescription refills. If this isn't enough for a day's work, the primary care physician still has to collaborate with colleagues in the practice, monitor how the practice is doing with the medical group's practice manager, and talk with hospital staff who have additional expectations to fulfill administrative responsibilities like medical committee involvement, medical meetings and statistical reviews.

The same is true for the clinical nurse practitioner, who may have more time to talk with patients about their chronic pain, but still has a high patient caseload per day, similar electronic health record recording requirements and authorization requests, and the task of collaborating with the primary care physician about the specific needs of each patient.

The physician assistant or medical assistant helps the primary care practitioner and clinical nurse practitioner take a patient's vital signs and review patient medication lists. There is little time to talk much with each patient, given the assistant's caseload.

It's easy to understand why these healthcare providers are so overwhelmed and stressed out to the maximum. They can burn out easily, yet they have major responsibilities and are held accountable to evaluate and treat all their patients, especially those patients who may have greater demands -- including those with chronic pain.

This is why the trained mental health clinician is a critical team member, someone who helps guide each patient towards living a healthier pain management lifestyle. The on- or off-site mental health clinician should have more time to do this (if you don't), given the time constraints of most healthcare providers. The responsibilities of this trained team member should include the following:

1. Assess the patient's perspectives or beliefs about their chronic pain and evaluate the ways they are trying to deal with it.
2. Teach the patient how to measure their pain levels over time using the five pain scales (see Chapter 5).
3. Help determine the patient's motivation to change the methods they are using to reduce their pain levels. This implies helping the patient identify the advantages and disadvantages of continuing to use, or changing, their present methods of reducing their pain levels.
4. Help the patient grieve or mourn the loss of the way they were before having chronic pain, or the way they would like to be again.
5. Help the patient reframe how ongoing pain reduction and maintenance can be viewed as a challenge, rather than as a catastrophe or major loss.
6. Help the patient choose a Pain Management Lifestyle by identifying their individualized S.M.A.R.T. goals and sub-goals and specific ways they choose to reduce their chronic pain over time.
7. Serve as a check-in coach to monitor how the patient is doing over time. This includes helping the patient learn to recognize triggers so as to prevent relapses.

8. Collaborate with the other primary pain management team members and auxiliary healthcare specialists to review the patient's progress using the Pain Management Lifestyle Model over time.

While the pain management team serves as the main medical component to help patients monitor their chronic pain, the sub-component extension of the team can include a variety of healthcare providers: surgeons, physiatrists, and neurologists; rheumatologists and endocrinologists; physical, rehabilitation, and occupational therapists; chiropractors, nutritionists, acupuncturists, and massage therapists; and a number of other professionals eager to help treat the patient for their chronic pain. What's most important is the need for ongoing collaboration and communication by the specialists with the primary pain management team including the mental health clinician. I also recognize the potential utility of a pastoral counselor or spiritual advisor, as my intent with this model is to help those with physical pain improve their level of gratitude, love, and spirituality.

Although most chronic pain patients prefer to receive services from their primary pain management team, many more of them are being referred directly to pain management centers. These centers are similar to the pain management team, although the primary physician at such centers is typically an anesthesiologist who specializes in pain medicine. The remaining members of the team are similar to those who are part of the patient's primary pain management team and may include a trained mental health clinician who can perform similar responsibilities as the ones described above.

The American Academy of Pain Medicine noted in a December 2016 paper that chronic pain patients may be referred to a specific pain management center if their primary pain management team member feels uncomfortable continuing their patient's current treatment; if a specific procedure is indicated (e.g., low back pain with radiculopathy), or if there is clear evidence of medication misuse or abuse.

A 2011 study of Canadian family physicians indicated that they typically refer patients to pain clinics directly when there is a specific request for nerve blocks or other injections; when there is a clear desire for the expertise of the program staff, or when their family physician has concerns about prescribing opioids. Patients won't be referred if the pain clinic has a long waiting list or there is a direct preference for other types of treatments.

Many more primary care physicians are referring patients directly to pain centers because of their concerns about having the frequency of their opioid prescriptions compared to the frequency of similar physicians based on their participation in prescription drug monitoring programs (PDMPs). Physicians don't want to be scrutinized by federal and state officials who monitor their opioid prescriptions. The same is true for surgeons, specialists like neurologists and physiatrists, and clinical nurse practitioners. Consequently, more pain medicine specialists are having difficulty prescribing opioids because they, too, don't want to fall above the mean for opioid prescriptions compared to other pain specialists. The need for alternatives to opioids increases substantially as a result of the continuing referrals to these centers. It's no wonder that specific pain management centers can have long waiting lists.

To summarize, the best way to reduce your stress as a critical member of the pain management team is to do the following:

- Be realistic about your expectations! While you only have a short time to see each one of your patients, know that you still make a difference in helping them reduce their pain over time.
- Always think of establishing S.M.A.R.T. sub-goals (discussed in Chapter 3).
- Realize that there is no one cure for your patients' pain.
- Reframe the word "pain" as a new paradigm that involves pain from life stress, emotions, negative thinking and lack of fortitude.
- Reframe the word "chronic" as "intermittent and ongoing."
- Recognize that there are two stages to managing pain: pain reduction and pain maintenance over time.
- Maintain confidence that you can offer each patient hope that you can help them (no matter how much you think is "good enough").
- You have the support of others because you are one member of a collaborating pain management team.
- Learn the ten facts about chronic pain presented in Chapter 3.
- Learn about the Pain Management Lifestyle Model presented in Chapter 4.
- Learn about the five pain management scales you can use to monitor pain reduction change over time (see Chapter 5.) While these scales assess a lot of information, they can easily be given to your patients to take home to self-monitor their pain levels over time.
- Learn about ways to help patients improve each of their pain scale ratings (discussed in Chapters 7 through 12).
- If you believe this is too much for you to do, then enlist the collaborative help of the mental health clinician trained in this model and who is a critical member of your pain management team.

Whatever your experience has been as a healthcare provider in treating patients with chronic pain, please realize that you are not alone. If anything, it is my intention to restore your hope that you and your colleagues can reduce your patients' levels of chronic pain, first, by accepting ten facts about chronic pain that are common to every patient who experiences it; second, by understanding the Pain Management Lifestyle Model; and third, by encouraging each of your patients to use the strategies for implementing a Pain Management Lifestyle, so they can reduce their chronic pain. As well, it is my hope to reduce your stress level by introducing the possibility that you may change your expectations for your chronic pain patients, and for yourself as a healthcare professional. Let's move on to the ten key facts about chronic pain.

Catching facts proved difficult for slow-footed Melvin.

Chapter 3: Ten Facts About Chronic Pain

Whatever your patients' experience has been, they may realize that they are not alone in having chronic pain. A first step in successfully working with your patients to reduce their levels of chronic pain is helping them accept ten facts about chronic pain that are common to everyone who has it.

Ten Facts About Chronic Pain

1. Chronic pain isn't new -- the intensity of the pain is.
2. Chronic pain is subjective.
3. Each patient with chronic pain is different.
4. Pain is multi-dimensional.
5. Your patients may always have chronic pain.
6. Some coping strategies your patients use are better than others.
7. Your patients must learn to "let go" of the way they were before having chronic pain.
8. Patients with chronic pain differ in their motivation to change.
9. Times are changing rapidly.
10. Each patient is free to determine what is in their best interest to reduce their chronic pain.

Fact #1: Chronic Pain Has a Different Intensity.

Pain is not new for any patient having it chronically. It's just that the intensity of it is different.

Like other human beings, each patient of yours has experienced pain since infancy. Often, it's a positive sign that indicated they were hurting; that they needed help; that they were hungry, tired or needed a new diaper. As each patient aged, they were pained that something was hurting. They had experienced pain from temporary separations, losses or rejections. Often, pain was seen as an opportunity to self-soothe, grow, learn to deal with disappointments and frustrations, and to delay gratification by confronting life challenges. Most of your patients have experienced all kinds of emotional pain like anxiety, sadness, or anger, and had the ability to reduce their pain by learning language, by saying or doing things that made them relieved. They had pain from life stressors, many of which they had no control over, but recovered from them.

With the advent of neural development, there was pain that your patients developed from their faulty thinking or cognitive distortions emanating from executive functions of their prefrontal cortex and other associated areas of their brains responsible for determining cognitive appraisals. Of most concern were your patients' difficulties in developing higher-level functioning skills like problem-solving, cognitive shifting or the ability to change their way of thinking and self-monitoring, or what psychologists have revealed as an "observing self." The philosopher Immanuel Kant wrote that, "Man is distinguished above all animals by his self-consciousness, by which he is a 'rational animal.'"

Your patients further learned how to cope with pain in many ways to build their self-esteem, optimism and resilience. Their pain may have increased from not meeting high, self-imposed standards or by becoming preoccupied with obsessive worries over situations they found uncontrollable or which they were helpless to change. Their pain could have come from feeling too much bitterness or guilt, or too little love or affection. They could have much pain from abuse.

When your patients have too much pain, their neurological structures become oversensitized. The threshold for tolerating even the slightest touches or pressures can be painful, as in your patients who have fibromyalgia, osteoarthritis or various musculoskeletal disorders. This is called central sensitization. C. Woolf noted that "Nociceptor inputs can trigger a prolonged but reversible increase in the excitability and synaptic efficacy of neurons in central nociceptive pathways." A person can feel pain in many places, at different times.

Another major factor to consider is the genetic predisposition of each patient to a specific body system or systems that can become vulnerable to attack or dysfunction when their immune system is lowered for any reason, especially when they're experiencing constant stress. In my family, for example, there is a strong genetic predisposition to musculoskeletal disorders. In other families, it may be cardiovascular disorders, while in others, it may be gastrointestinal, endocrine, dermatological or neurological disorders. Whichever systems are vulnerable, your patients should be made aware of their predispositions so as to monitor potential symptoms carefully, especially those than can increase their chronic pain.

Your patients have the capability to reduce their pain levels neurologically by utilizing the different strategies I'll recommend later in the book that can alter their neural pathways in positive ways. This is called "neuroplasticity," a term dating as far back as 1890, used by author and psychologist William James.

Fact #2: Chronic Pain is Subjective.

Every one of your patient's experiences of their chronic pain is unique and different from every other one of your patient's experiences. Each patient has different physical perceptions of pain, based on their levels of hypersensitivity and pain thresholds. For example, why is it that one of your patients can't walk fifty feet while another patient can hike mountain trails, even though both have the same level of disc degeneration or bulges in their discs at the same vertebrae levels? Why can one of your patients with moderate stenosis do gardening while another patient with the same condition can't even bend down? Multiple factors contribute to each patient's experience of pain.

Fact #3: Each Patient with Chronic Pain is Different.

A patient's perception is influenced by genetic predisposition, temperament, and a given organ system's vulnerability to stress. Each person's brain segments grow at different rates; this is especially true for the frontal lobe, which is responsible for higher-level executive functions. This area is similar to the computer processor that regulates how a car functions. A car's fuel injector is similar to the part of the brain called the limbic system. Each person has different early developmental experiences in achieving major milestones in speech and fine and gross motor development. Exposure to different parenting styles influences a person's growth, as do sibling order, family and friend interactions, schooling, and cultural background. Early experiences of trauma, like physical or sexual abuse, can have a markedly high impact on a person's ability to cope with pain.

Pain Management Lifestyle:

The ability to choose ongoing specific thoughts,
emotions and actions that help you to foster resilience when
you are challenged by chronic pain.

The ability to reduce your chronic pain using the 5 pain scales over time.

Fact #4: Pain is Multi-Dimensional.

Your patient's pain is generated in many ways. There is the physical pain that the medical community only measures by asking, "On a scale of 1 to 10, what is your level of pain right now?" But what about your patient's cognitive or thinking pain, based on faulty appraisals of situations in their past, or based on negative self-talk? Then there's your patient's emotional pain, such as having different levels of depression, anxiety, anger and happiness. Each person's unique appraisal of pain comes from experiencing different life stressors at different times. Each of your patients may have different strengths that allow them to deal with pain -- like coping, self-care, self-efficacy or experiencing mastery of completing tasks, assertiveness, optimism, resilience, gratitude, love and spirituality. All these dimensions contribute to their ability to lower or raise their pain levels. Consequently, your patients must measure and self-monitor their pain levels, even on a weekly basis.

Fact #5: Your Patients May Always Have Chronic Pain.

This may be the toughest one for your patients to accept, since any level of physical pain lasting longer than three months is considered "chronic." Each patient may like to believe that their physical pain can be eliminated once and for all, but this won't happen because we're describing multiple contributors to pain that impact each patient at different times.

This fact may be especially helpful for you as a healthcare provider, in that it can help you to lower your self-standards and stop believing that there is one miracle solution or cure for total pain elimination.

Like me, I'm sure you've read and heard enough from professionals and advertisements that "guarantee" total relief from chronic pain, or even a total cure, from one treatment modality.

I'll never forget several years ago, I was having lunch with a friend at a local Italian restaurant where we were discussing a particular person we both knew who had stage III or IV cancer. No sooner had we begun to discuss this than a chiropractor who was sitting alone behind us and had been eavesdropping, got up from his seat and shared how his chiropractic techniques could be a "cure-all" for any type of cancer, not to mention any medical condition under the sun. Perhaps the most painful aspect of this professional's affirmations was that he had a thriving practice by virtue of using incredible marketing tools and by his powerful use of therapeutic persuasion to convince patients that they could eliminate, not reduce, any known medical condition. He happened to have a large office on the first floor of the same professional building I was in and I would often pass by and see dozens of patients sitting in multiple rooms, waiting to be treated by the chiropractor or by one of his colleagues. There was not even any clear ethical consideration for patient confidentiality, since any passerby could see all the patients through uncurtained glass windows. As well, there were multiple marketing posters lining the exterior walls of his chiropractic practice, offering free seminars and free initial consultations.

Please don't get me wrong! I am not generalizing that all chiropractors, or all physicians, surgeons or physical therapists, or even psychologists, practice in this manner. This would be a clear cognitive error on my part, no different than the all-or-nothing thinking that I will discuss later on in Chapter 5.

Still, the power of persuasion and belief is incredible. Just look up how many books (print and audio), DVDs, CDs, articles and podcasts you can find on any subject. People will believe anything, especially if they are vulnerable to certain conditions and are not willing to take the time to examine someone's credentials, education and training or the research on any particular treatment modality. Just consider the power of the placebo effect or marketing strategy that urges a patient to call a 1-800 number to "hurry fast and get this ___ for only $___. Act now and you will also get ____."

I must humbly admit that I might appear to be doing the same thing by asking you to believe that I am offering you this new model to help you reduce your patients' chronic pain. But, unlike some other ill-trained, inexperienced professionals, or those who generate superficial marketing techniques (like the chiropractor who promised that his chiropractic treatment can cure cancer), I hope that I am, at least, providing you with my professional and personal background to help you decide, as a medical professional, if my information is worth reading.

Instead of trying to rid themselves of their pain once and for all, the goals of patients who suffer from chronic pain should be to reduce their negative ratings on the specific pain scales included in this book that measure increased pain, and to improve their positive ratings on scales that show reduced pain, over time. (We'll talk more about these scales in Chapter 5). This is very similar to the relapse prevention techniques used for patients who are trying to lose weight and then maintain realistic weight ranges, or diabetics watching their blood sugar levels, or people trying to reduce or eliminate their use of substances like opioids, alcohol or tobacco.

Some Maladaptive Coping Strategies

Staying in Bed

Blaming others

Controlling others

Fact #6: Some Coping Strategies Are Better Than Others.

There are different ways to cope with having chronic pain. Some are much better than others. If you see any of your patients using these ineffective coping strategies, try to have them stop and find more beneficial ones. (See Chapters 7 through 12 for specific ideas.)

Avoid: Your patients stay away from taking any action that can help them reduce chronic pain. This can simply be staying in bed all day, thinking it's better to just lie there under the covers and escape from experiencing any pain. They might avoid seeing family or friends, or they may have frequent appointment cancellations or no-shows.

Rationalize: Your patients come up with all sorts of reasons to not do anything to reduce their chronic pain.

Cover Up: Your patients cover up their feelings by drinking excessively, smoking more cigarettes, eating compulsively or relying exclusively on opiates.

Anxiety, Depression and Anger: Your patients become more anxious, depressed or angry.

Regress: Your patients regress, acting like children who are demanding, throwing tantrums, crying constantly, or dependent.

Blame: Your patients blame others for their continuing to have chronic pain, making them feel less worthy because they've never experienced it. They often blame you for being a healthcare professional who can't supply them with the "perfect cure."

Play the Victim: Your patients become victims, seek negative attention and pity, increase their physician visits, or become disabled. (This last one is a strong guilt-inducer.)

Control Others: Your patients may use their chronic pain symptoms to exert control over their relationships, including relationships with family members and healthcare professionals. Chronic pain symptoms can be very powerful in persuading others to give in to your patient's needs.

Defending

CONSEQUENCE OF MAKING MALADAPTIVE CHOICES
("Stuckness" - Defeatism)

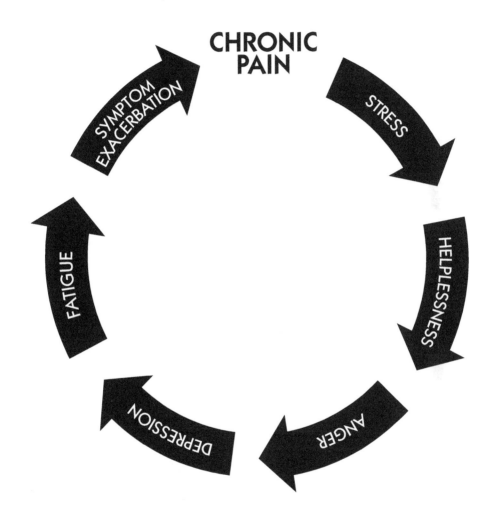

CHRONIC PAIN

STRESS

HELPLESSNESS

ANGER

DEPRESSION

FATIGUE

SYMPTOM EXACERBATION

Fact #7: Your Patients Must Let Go of
"The Way They Were" Before Having Chronic Pain.

A critical stage for your patients to work through is grieving, or letting go of, the way they were before they had chronic pain.

Your patients can't change the fact that they were given certain challenges, but they can certainly learn from them. Who said life is fair? It rarely is. Who said mourning isn't healthy? It tests your patients' capacities to build their own resilience. All hope isn't lost. Your patients may need to lower their standards if they think grieving isn't an acceptable way to cope with loss. Your patients should reappraise grieving or "letting go" as a challenge or an opportunity to grow. Even trees lose their leaves in the fall to make new ones in the spring. Perennial flowers wither only to blossom the next year, more beautiful than before.

The late physician and author Elizabeth Kubler-Ross identified five stages of grief that can help your patients accept their losses rather than remain stuck in denial or continuing sadness. While Dr. Ross identified the five stages as denial, anger, bargaining, depression, and acceptance, she did not assume people would go through each stage with equal intensity or experience each stage just like others do.

Grief stages may not have a clear progression. Still, each stage has its characteristics. For example, if you have a patient who experienced a major trauma like a serious injury from a car accident, she might first experience shock, disbelief, and a numbing of feelings. She may enter some dreamlike state or escape into fantasy about not having pain. She may even turn to alcohol or drugs to dull her pain. Being angry about having chronic pain is real. Your patients can be angry at you, their healthcare professional, who might have misdiagnosed their condition or might have given them poor advice. They may be angry at you because you couldn't prescribe the perfect solution to eliminate their chronic pain. Your patients can be angry at those who love them for not knowing what it's like to have their pain. They can even get angry at G-d or some higher power they believe in. No matter who or what they're angry with or about, the feeling doesn't take away their pain. They may not realize it at the time, but their anger may be pushing away the most important people in their lives who love and care about them.

They may want to bargain with G-d or a higher power to get rid of the pain. They may seek greater control of it by going from one healthcare provider to another, demanding more of each provider, looking for the right answer to allow them to go back to the way they were before the pain began.

They may focus a great deal on what they could have done to prevent the pain from occurring. They may feel much guilt and regret for being careless in situations that they thought they had no control over. A greater conflict is for them to be thinking about how life could be if they didn't have chronic pain.

It's normal for patients to become depressed when they are mourning their old life free of pain. They may feel so alone that they think no one cares. Their closest family and friends may not understand what they're going through because they never experienced chronic pain. The loss of their previous lives can be so intense that patients may become so depressed that they think it's not worth living anymore. Feelings of helplessness and hopelessness may overwhelm them to the point that they can't move without experiencing pain. They cry, even sob at times, longing to return to those days when they thought nothing about ever having chronic pain. This stage is of critical concern for you as a healthcare professional, given the higher risk of suicide for chronic pain patients (when compared to the general population) and what I call "passive suicide" like opiate or alcohol dependence, obesity or simply nonadherence to treatment.

Your patients can't begin to reduce their chronic pain unless they complete this mourning phase. In her book *Necessary Losses*, author Judith Viorst describes how each of us encounters painful situations throughout life. Your patients need to let go of idealistic or unrealistic expectations that all their pain will eventually be gone. You can see why we're talking not only of physical pain, but of emotional pain, of pain from life stressors, faulty thinking or lack of fortitude. Does this sound like a tough one? Well, it is! No one likes to be told that it is a more realistic goal to reduce their pain than to be totally free of all pain.

Acknowledge
MOURNING – GRIEVING – LETTING GO
"The way one was" vs. "the way one wants to be"
vs. "the way one is"

Shock/Denial –
Pain/Guilt
Depression/Reflection
Loneliness

Moving Forward
Reconstruction/
Working Through
Acceptance and Hope

Receive — Reflect --- Accept --- Adapt

Fact #8: Patients with Chronic Pain Differ in their Motivation to Change.

James Prochaska and Carlo C. DiClemente (1983) designed a "motivation to change" model that is still used today to determine patients' motivation to change their thoughts, feelings and actions. The model implies that your patients move through a progressive series of stages, each of which requires different tasks. While it is assumed that a patient progresses from one stage to the next, the authors acknowledge that a patient can begin at any stage and can move back and forth between stages at any time because of relapses.

The stages of change include the following:

- Pre-contemplation (Denial)
- Contemplation (Ambivalence)
- Determination (Commitment)
- Action (Participation)
- Maintenance (Continuity)

Let's look at each of these stages one by one.

Pre-Contemplation (or Denial) Stage

If your patients are in the pre-contemplation stage, they may deny that there is sufficient reason to change their behavior. They avoid change because they believe their present strategies to deal with pain are good enough, or they're sure someone else thinks they have more of a problem coping with chronic pain than they do. They have no thoughts about changing even if their coping strategies are unhealthy, like staying in bed; not exercising; or drinking, eating, or smoking excessively. They believe they have tried to change their present ways of dealing with pain with little to no benefit. They don't view any alternative strategies as effective, based on their past experiences.

In fact, they resist changing their behaviors because the benefits of continuing the strategies they are using to cope with chronic pain outweigh the negative ones. For example, your patient may rationalize that it doesn't matter whether they take walks or go regularly to physical therapy. Perhaps they may say something like, "What's the use? My pain's not going away" or "At least I feel relief when I lie down." They can justify maintaining these strategies and they believe they are doing enough to cope as best as they can. If they're depressed, they experience even more reasons to do less. They're aware others may never understand what chronic pain is like because they've never had it.

If your patients have increased levels of anxiety, they are clear that remaining at home gives them greater security and comfort than going to the mall for a walk or driving to physical therapy appointments. If they get panic attacks or fear uncontrollable situations, then there are greater benefits to them in avoiding going out. Martin Seligman identified this condition as "learned helplessness." When your patients believe that whatever they do will only sustain chronic pain, they will give up trying to change to make it better. They will become depressed, and stick to what they are doing.

Sustaining high levels of chronic pain can be worthwhile for some of your patients. There are unrecognized advantages to not changing their present strategies to cope with chronic pain. For example, they can remain depressed because it can be one of the only ways they have to get other people's attention and concern. Having continued pain can be a way to avoid household responsibilities or to control what others say or do around them at home or when out with friends. They can blame their chronic pain on others or come up with multiple reasons why they should not change their pain levels. They can maintain high levels of pain to get disability insurance or to file a lawsuit against a person or an institution.

I'll never forget the maladaptive strategies used by a person with whom I played tennis. He obtained Social Security Disability because he claimed he was too depressed to cope with an impending divorce. That person wound up selling merchandise "under the table" (meaning the income was hidden from normal reporting and taxation), purchased two ski condominiums, skied every winter, and continued to play tennis, all year long. His presumed depression paid off.

A man came to see me because he was allegedly having severe panic attacks. When I asked what he had tried in the past, he offered a litany of strategies, all of which "never worked." After just two sessions, he never returned, claiming that he wanted to reduce his attacks but seemed reluctant to follow recommendations. Two weeks later, I received a letter from his attorney, asking for a full report on the patient's condition because he had an appeal hearing coming up with the disability board. The "patient" had never wanted to change his condition. His attorney simply told him to see a psychologist to obtain more credible information to help his appeal. I refused and wrote to the attorney that the patient was a malingerer.

Don't get me wrong. There are many people who truly have chronic pain that impedes their ability to work and enjoy life. They deserve disability insurance. For example, a middle-aged female school administrator was referred to me for an evaluation and therapy after sustaining a hard fall from a rickety school ladder, injuring her left arm and wrist and rendering her incapable of performing administrative tasks. This patient had a clear desire to return to work, missed not being at her school job, and became increasingly depressed. She saw a specialized orthopedic surgeon, had hand surgery, then went for physical therapy. Both the surgeon and physical therapist informed the patient that her physical recovery would take a long time due to the complexity of her multiple hand and wrist injuries. While she chose to file for disability, she had to grieve the loss because she had a strong work ethic.

Prochaska and DiClemente wrote that a patient's pre-contemplation resistance to change can be identified as one of the "4 Rs": reluctance, rebellion, rationalization and resignation. If your patient is a reluctant pre-contemplator, they either lack knowledge or simply don't want to change. Your patient may

41

be fearful or reluctant to risk the discomfort of change. If they are a rebellious pre-contemplator, your patient may know why s/he doesn't want to change but doesn't like being pressured or told what to do. They may like to argue with you or other healthcare providers or caring others, giving all kinds of reasons to not change. If your patient's a rationalizing pre-contemplator, they may come up with all kinds of excuses to not change. They minimize harm and have difficulty thinking about the benefits of any change. Finally, if your patient is a resigned pre-contemplator, they give up and do nothing to change because they believe nothing else will improve their condition (learned helplessness).

If you are on the pain management team or are an extended healthcare provider, the best kind of help for you to provide is consciousness-raising or increasing your patient's awareness by giving them educational information about their condition. Your patient needs others to be sensitive and understanding about why they may not want to change, especially if it means listening to their sadness in grieving what they have lost or the benefits of feeling relief from simply lying in bed. Your patient may want others to accept and empathize with what they are saying while understanding that the decision to change or not to change is totally up to them, even if it may be against your professional advice. Your patient wants you to validate their lack of readiness and to discuss how their current behaviors are influenced by their thoughts and feelings about changing, without your being judgmental. Your patient wants you to affirm that the decision to change is up to them, even if you realize how difficult it is for them to change.

What you may *not* want to do for someone who is at this stage of change is to respond, as you perhaps were trained to do, with direct advice or by trying to persuade your patient to change their maladaptive choices. You may need to withhold lectures or try not to react to your patient with frustration, irritability, impatience or anger. If they are rebellious, you may want to avoid struggling. Your professional expertise is not being questioned here.

If anything, you want to try to understand what would make your patient be reluctant, rebellious, rationalizing or resigned to resisting change. In other words, you may want to join with your patient for the time being; don't take their resistance to change personally. Your willingness to understand and tactfully educate them about chronic pain and what you know about their choices in the short and long term can prove to be invaluable.

Contemplation Stage

In the contemplation stage, your chronic pain patient becomes more serious in their thinking about change. They acknowledge there is a problem and they weigh the pros and cons about change, but they don't yet commit to any action. Instead, your patient gathers more information and is open to further explanation of alternative strategies, weighing their short- and long-term consequences. Often, it is very helpful for someone on the pain management team to help the patient rate each reason for and against change on a scale of 1 to 5, with 1 being a not very important concern and 5 being a very important concern. Your patient ends up with two scores. For the first score, have your patient count the number of advantages and the number of disadvantages related to change. For the second score, add up all the ratings on each side and compare them. This second score is the comparative total weighted values of all the ratings on each side from 1-5.

You may help your patient gain additional information from important others when doing a sort of cost-benefit analysis of change. You may want to accentuate the positive reasons to change their strategies for reducing pain and improving their quality of life. It may be important for them to hear your perspectives about their reasons and the weights attached to them, for and against change, especially in the long term.

This stage is particularly important to work through if your patient with chronic pain tends to become anxious often and worries constantly about what to do differently to reduce their pain. Constant worry can lead your patient to remain paralyzed in this stage. Realize it is the next stage, the action stage, that will bring pain relief to your chronic pain patient.

I am still surprised that so many healthcare practitioners continue to give advice or just prescribe a medication for a patient's chronic pain without considering that the patient may still be in a pre-contemplative or contemplative stage of change.

Here's an Example:

Your patient John is overweight and has severe chronic pain. He doesn't want to go for his yearly physical because the last few times he went, all he could remember was that his medical practitioner told him what to do about his weight. But his wife Selma demanded that he go, so John scheduled an appointment and reluctantly went to the office.

After the initial check-in routine and ten-minute wait, there was a knock on the door. "Good afternoon, John. It's great you see you again! I know you've been expressing concerns about your constant pain, so I'm here to check you over thoroughly today." John nodded in agreement. The medical practitioner then checked John thoroughly and said, "You know, John, I'm very concerned about your weight and the impact it has on your pain levels.

43

Listen! I want you to get into a structured exercise routine and see my colleague who runs a nutrition program." John agreed.

Eventually, John got dressed and went home. His wife asked, "How did it go?"

"Great!" John said happily. "The practitioner told me that I'm doing fine. My weight is okay and I don't have to come back until next year."

Imagine how much further the practitioner could have gotten if he or she said something like, "Look, John, I understand that it's difficult to commit to anything right now. So, why don't we do this? Let me give you some additional information about the relationship between chronic pain and weight. How about after reading this, you make a list on a sheet of paper of all the reasons you don't want to do anything about your weight. On the other side, list all the reasons why you may want to do some things about it and indicate the degree of importance each reason has for you on a scale of 1 to 5, and let's see what you get."

Preparation Stage

Next, in the preparation stage, your patient has reviewed all the costs and benefits of change and is now 100% committed to action. At this point, you can help your patient design strategies to improve their condition, but don't yet put them into action.

Goal-setting is a major priority at this stage. You can help your patient make a list of potential goals that would be the most realistic for them to try to achieve. To reduce frustration and disappointment, your patient should try to establish goals that are specific and realistically attainable within identified time periods. If your patient's goals are aimed too high, then you can help them divide their goals into sub-goals (action steps) to fit the reality of your patient's condition. This is especially true if your patient is a perfectionist with high self-standards he or she has difficulty lowering. They may find it somewhat anxiety-provoking and painful to let go of what they could do in the past, but consider the price they pay for struggling to maintain such high standards, especially if they have been a high achiever and performed exceptionally well in certain areas before they had chronic pain. It is best for you to help your patient establish realistic short- and long-term goals so that they become less frustrated and disappointed.

Let's say your patient John (from the example above) decided to do what you advised and realized that he needed to make that 100% commitment to change. To help himself lose weight, he wrote down the following goals and sub-goals:

1. Eat healthy

A. Have a nutritionist help me get to a better weight range.
B. Establish a healthy amount of weight to lose each month.
C. Buy and eat only healthy foods.
D. Weigh myself each day in the morning.
E. Have Selma and two friends support me in my efforts
    to lose weight, then maintain a healthy weight range over time.

2. Exercise

A. Walk each day, starting at 15 minutes. Increase gradually to 1 hour.
B. Join the local gym and go there at least 3 times weekly.
C. Write down positive self-coping statements to confront all
    my reasons to avoid exercising.

Once your patient has their goals written down, you can help them evaluate these goals. You may ask them questions like these: How important is it that you achieve these goals and what are the reasons? Are your goals written in positive ways? For example, "I will improve my health and feel less pain if I lose X pounds in X months" is much more positive than "I will lose weight so I don't feel like such a fat loser." Are your goals realistic, given your pain condition? Could you divide a large goal into smaller action steps to be taken within a specific time frame? Are your standards too high? How will you know that you have reached your goals?

Use the S.M.A.R.T. model when helping your chronic pain patient write down their goals. Put simply, a S.M.A.R.T goal is defined as one that is specific, measurable, achievable, results-focused, and time-bound.

- **Specific:** Goals should clearly define what your patient will do,
  why they will want to do it, and how they will do it.
  Example: *"I will lose 50 pounds, then maintain a healthy weight
  range over time to help relieve my leg pain. I will do this by
  eating in a healthy way and by exercising a minimum of 15 to 35
  minutes each day."*

- **Measurable:** Goals should be measurable so that your patient
  has clear evidence that they have accomplished them.
  Example: *"I will know that I have lost 50 pounds by weighing myself
  each morning and comparing the result to my baseline
  weight of 255 pounds."*

- **Achievable:** Goals should be attainable. They should be realistic and based on your patient's knowledge, skills, and abilities. **Example:** *"I have identified 50 pounds as a realistic amount to lose and, if necessary, I will modify my time frame monthly after discussing my progress with my nutritionist."*

- **Results-Focused:** Goals should have measured outcomes. **Example:** *"I will know I have lost enough weight when I lose 50 pounds."*

- **Time-bound:** Goals should be linked to a reasonable time frame. **Example:** *"I will lose at least 50 pounds in 6 months. I will remain within +/- 5 pounds of my goal at the end of each consecutive month."*

Here are some other goals your patient with chronic pain may want to consider:

- Identify the triggers that increase their pain.
- Get between 7 to 9 hours of restful sleep per night.
- Identify 10 positive coping statements they may say to reduce their pain.
- List the positive consequences of being at the action stage of change.
- List 10 ways to care for themselves.

When your patient is considering specific, realistic goals, have them write down the following:

"I will _____by (time frame)_____."

If your patient with chronic pain is in the preparation stage, you will want to help them gather information about different strategies that would be in their best interests. Your patient should take time to research this as best as they can. They should educate themselves about what resources are available, ranging from books and online information to recommendations from you and other members of their pain management team and other specialists, all to help them prepare what they will want to try first.

Prochaska and DiClemente's Transtheoretical Stages of Change Model

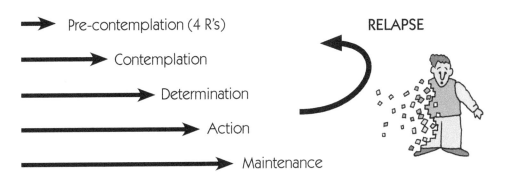

Pre-contemplation (4 R's)

Contemplation

Determination

Action

Maintenance

RELAPSE

Motivational Techniques To Enhance Change

Express empathy

Develop discrepancy

Avoid argumentation

Roll with resistance

Support self-efficacy

Adapted from materials by W. Miller and S. Rollnick

Action Stage

The next motivation-to-change state, the action stage, is where your patient can most improve their self-esteem and reduce their chronic pain. Action brings your patient ultimate pain relief. It is the doing, not the excessive thinking or worrying, that will bring them the most satisfaction and pleasure. In this stage, your patient experiences results.

Each patient's strategies to reduce their chronic pain will be different. They can be modified at any time, depending on whether your patient experiences continuing success or encounters too many obstacles. The key is for you, as one of their healthcare providers, to help your patient to not lose hope. Help them make changes and adjust their course of action as needed.

It can be very helpful to make sure your patient has a significant other in their life to be a coach or cheerleader or someone else who is also taking action to reduce their own chronic pain. From a healthcare perspective, this person may be someone like you who offers them ongoing encouragement and who collaborates with them and their significant other to help with self-monitoring as your patient pursues their specific pain reduction strategies. You can provide your patient with feedback to help them consider whether their goals and sub-goals are still realistic or whether they need to be modified.

Maintenance Stage

Finally, when your patient with chronic pain is in the maintenance stage, they are continuing to act on their chosen strategies and are helped by you to be aware of any triggers that might cause them to relapse to an earlier stage. This maintenance stage is the most crucial of all because it is ongoing and vital for long-term change. Too many of your patients pursue strategies to reduce their chronic pain but don't consider the importance of long-term commitment and the possibility of regressing to previous stages because they experience too little in the way of results. For example, you may find that many of your patients who have acted on their goals have reduced their chronic pain to a low pain range, but once they get there, their pain levels go back up because they are not fully committed. To prevent relapse, you may want to help patients pay attention to their thinking and to the emotional and physical triggers that can set them back. You can help your patient self-monitor these signals, as can other supportive people in your patient's network, especially the person designated by your patient as a caretaker.

Maintaining a long-term commitment to a Pain Management Lifestyle means your patient must recognize that there will be bumps in the road. They must try to do everything it takes to accept this, so they don't become frustrated and disappointed, then regress to and remain at an earlier stage. This is why I recommend that your patient continues to use pain scale ratings during the maintenance phase of change, to help reduce their chronic pain long-term.

Fact #9: Times Are Changing Rapidly.

We are witnessing, almost daily, an exponential increase in technological advancements that make it easier to get information and direct activities simply by pushing a button or speaking into a built-in cellphone microphone. While these developments are mostly positive, they have created inherent negative side effects that we can see in individuals ranging from young children to adults. Some of these include an inability to delay gratification, tolerate frustration and boredom, be patient and/or think critically. We are not being taught or relearning these skills as rapidly as the technology changes. Even adults are questioning whether they have undiagnosed Attention Deficit Hyperactivity Disorder (primarily inattentive, hyperactive, impulsive or combined) because of sudden, previously undiscovered problems handling multitask demands. Many individuals are experiencing increased anxiety while others are turning towards addictions if they can't keep up with technological advancements. Many want a quick answer or one ultimate, pain-relieving treatment, like a prescription, that will totally alleviate their pain once and for all.

The need for immediate gratification and the loss of patience have both risen to such an extent that they have impacted people's neurological condition, including the demand for brain structures to generate more of the neurotransmitter dopamine and changes in human brain structure, like the shrinkage of the hippocampus.

It's much like if your patient races their car's engine too much, or they stop and go too fast, they're going to "burn out" their car's engine and other crucial parts.

Many people, especially those in the baby boomer generation (like me), who were very athletic and exercised daily, were either not informed properly about long-term health risks or were simply not willing to change their exercise regime due to their inability to "let go" and accept change and loss, based on conflicts between high self- and societal expectations and standards and loss due to aging.

Even younger people are driven too much by thinking they have to surpass their daily expectations by using activity trackers like Fitbits.

Doctors talk in hospital lunchrooms almost daily about how they are seeing more young patients for rotator cuff surgeries, knee replacements, torn

ACLs, and other sports injuries. Even cardiologists are more frequently seeing younger patients for stress, high blood pressure and high cholesterol readings. Look at the level of obesity in this country. Wouldn't you think that has an impact on your patients' chronic pain?

Many of your patients are having difficulty keeping up with the rapid technological changes because of the impact on their pre-frontal cortex, which is responsible for executive functioning capacities to multi-task, organize, be cognitively flexible, initiate action, and self-monitor.

Many patients are anxious about losing jobs due to changing technology. More companies are sending their employees home to work alone on their computers to save on structural, fixed costs, which is leading to your patients feeling more lonely and isolated.

Another critical concern that has contributed to your patients having increased chronic pain is their desensitization to heightened exposures to sex and aggression in all types of media, which compete fiercely to attract attention.

What is also very concerning is the impact of heightened sensationalism about reported sexual and physical abuse cases. Such news media coverage is impacting the ability of some patients to repress memories of earlier physical, sexual, or emotional abuse experienced when they were children or teenagers. The news media seems almost oblivious to the impact their coverage of these kinds of cases can have on people who have chronic pain and suffer from PTSD.

Clearly, your patients who have chronic pain are at a critical stage where they can enhance their executive functioning to keep up with advancing technology. They will need to improve their coping skills, problem-solving abilities, and capacities to self-reflect and think deliberately and critically. Learning to perceive one's chronic pain as a challenge rather than a catastrophe can help your patients become more resilient, patient, optimistic and loving towards others, and should help them fight off the ill effects of the tragedies and pessimistic viewpoints they may see every day online, on TV, or in newspapers and magazines.

Fact #10: Your Patients with Chronic Pain Always Have Free Choice to Determine What Is in Their Best Interests to Reduce It.

The methods your patients choose to reduce their chronic pain will be their best methods at the time, even if they aren't what your other patients may prefer. For example, one of your patients may find that the best ways to maintain their Pain Management Lifestyle is to see a chiropractor twice weekly, have a massage once in a while and walk with a friend twice a week, even if

"Pain Management Lifestyle"

Use the the 5 pain scales to monitor the use of any
combination of ways.....over time

(Any combination of the items listed below)
"One size does not fit all"

IN COLLABORATION WITH AN INTERDISCIPLINARY STAFF

Surgical Procedures: Trigger point injections, nerve blocks, epidural steroid and facet injections, neural ablation, implantable pumps, internal transcutaneous electronic nerve stimulator, surgery

Physical Treatments: Physical therapy, aquatic therapy, chiropractic treatment, orthotics, hot/cold compresses, stretching, exercise, work with a trainer, nutrition for weight loss and maintenance, yoga, tai chi, acupuncture, massage, biofeedback, diaphragmatic breathing, progressive muscle relaxation, herbology, refloxology

Medications: NSAIDS, acetaminophren , SSRIs, SSNRIs, TCAs, anticonvulsants, opioids, muscle relaxants, topical agents, medical marijuana

Eduation: Courses, seminars, workshops, webinars, CDs, DVDs, applications, podcasts, blogs, assertiveness training, promoting happiness skills, anger management, stress management, mindfulness meditation, visual imagery, the relaxation response

Therapy: Motivational interviewing, grief therapy, pain-scale usage and monitoring, cognitive therapy, behavior therapy, distraction, hypnosis, pet therapy, light therapy, aromatherapy, sound therapy, reiki, bibliotherapy-self-help workbooks, journaling, gardening, art therapy, music therapy

Alternative Ways: Spirituality, prayer, humor, dramatics, socialization

it means walking just a few blocks then stopping to rest, then walking another few blocks. Why is that better or worse than another one of your patients who comments regularly on a blog site, does some easy stretches when they get up in the morning, goes to Weight Watchers meetings and does a beginners' aquatic therapy group? Still another patient may find it helpful to practice yoga or tai chi, while another may benefit from meeting weekly for breakfast with a friend who also has chronic pain. Another may practice mindfulness meditation daily and find much pleasure in distracting himself from pain by playing the piano or guitar.

It's important for you, as a healthcare provider, to refrain from being judgmental or simply telling your patients "what is best" to help them reduce their chronic pain over the long term. It is more critical for you and others in each patient's life to be empathetic, to listen, and to share what everyone notices about how they are coping, in ways good or bad, with their chronic pain.

Choosing A "Pain Management Lifestyle"

Defend   or   **Acknowledge**

FREE CHOICE

Avoid
Rationalize
Cover Up
Anxiety
Depression and Anger
Regression
Blame
Play the Victim
Control Others

Mourn-grieve-let go how one was vs. how one is.

Accept reality.

Perceive pain as a "challenge" vs. a major loss, threat, catastrophe.

Emphasize resilience.

"Pain Management Lifestyle"

CHRONIC PAIN

STRESS

Relapse

HELPLESSNESS

SYMPTOM EXACERBATION

FATIGUE

DEPRESSION

ANGER

When it comes to pain relief, Miss Reduction puts her foot down.

Chapter 4: A Model to
Reduce Your Patients' Pain

My model for reducing pain grew from the standard question often asked by healthcare providers and by what's typically required by the electronic health record: "What is your level of (physical) pain on a scale from 1 to 10?" Given the subjective, multidimensional nature of pain, including multiple factors that contribute to your patients' pain, it is critical to assess and treat pain in a different way. The term "pain" should be perceived as a metaphor for all kinds of pain -- not just physical. This is not to diminish the physical aspects of your patients' pain and their desire to find a clear, physical reason and treatment for it. However, identifying pain triggers and reducing pain requires a holistic approach rather than homing in on one specific aspect, like a subjective description of physical pain.

To identify, treat and reduce each patient's chronic pain, you should collaborate with other members of the pain management team to assess your patient's medical conditions. Initially, if you are the primary care physician or clinical nurse practitioner, you'll discuss the reason for the patient's visit and will do all of the following:

- Review the patient's present physical symptoms

- Perform a thorough physical exam
- Determine whether your patient's physical pain is acute (experienced for less than three months) or chronic (experienced for more than three months)
- Request additional medical procedures (like X-rays, an MRI, blood or urine tests) to determine if there is a clear medical diagnosis.
- Refer the patient to a specialist, like a neurosurgeon or orthopedic surgeon, neurologist or physiatrist, if necessary.

Typically, the cause of acute pain is clear-cut, often resulting from a recent injury. Your patient's pain can be eliminated within a short time period unless a surgical procedure or a recommendation for ongoing physical or chiropractic treatment is required.

If the pain management team decides that your patient's pain is chronic and, in your team's professional opinion, does not have to be referred directly to a pain management clinic because of your limited time, discomfort with your knowledge, concern for treating with a specific treatment, opioid medication or for your patient's alleged substance abuse, then your patient should meet with the team member who is either a health psychologist, psychiatric social worker or licensed mental health counselor, thoroughly trained in pain management, including the contents of this book. This team member, who can be on-site or at another location, will take a developmental history, including how the patient has dealt with challenges about pain before, and then will get the patient's perspective about what they think is causing their chronic pain.

The mental health clinician on the pain management team can then introduce the patient to the Pain Management Lifestyle Model and can review with the patient how people typically acknowledge, or defend against, pain: the cycle of pain if a person chooses maladaptive ways to defend against it; and determine if the patient has fully grieved or mourned their losses since having chronic pain. If not, the clinician may want to help the patient grieve their losses by using Elizabeth Kubler-Ross' model, as reviewed in Chapter 3.

Finally, the mental health clinician can introduce the patient to the five Pain Scales and show the patient how to complete them to further assess their present and ongoing appraisal of pain in a multidimensional way. These pain scales assess and measure physical pain, life stress, emotional pain, negative thinking and fortitude. It would be helpful for everyone on the pain management team, including auxiliary healthcare providers, to become familiar with and learn how to use these scales to monitor the patient's pain-level changes over time. There are examples of these scales in Chapter 5, with more explanations as to how they can be used and what they measure.

Whether you are a member of the primary pain management team, work at a pain clinic, or are an auxiliary healthcare provider like a surgeon, physiatrist, neurologist, endocrinologist, physical and rehabilitation therapist, chiropractor, psychologist or counselor, you can help your patient imagine that they are the navigator in a jet cockpit, monitoring a series of dials that identify the jet engines' efficiency to travel a very long distance (the patient's life). Your patient will want to improve those systems that generate and maintain optimum performance, as indicated by each dial measurement. Each of the five dials (Pain Scales) measures your patient's physical pain, emotional pain, pain from life stress, cognitive appraisals, and your patient's fortitude (the ability of your patient to handle chronic pain).

While the following strategies may be the primary responsibility of the mental health clinician, it is still helpful for you, as any type of healthcare provider, to understand how to identify and help your patient move though each motivational stage of change.

After scoring and interpreting the five pain scales with your patient, determine what stage of motivational change they are in (as discussed in Chapter 3). If your patient is in a pre-contemplative stage of change, you may want to try to understand the short- and long-term consequences of their using certain maladaptive methods to deal with their chronic pain, then share what you know as a trained healthcare provider about chronic pain and its relevance to how your patient is trying to deal with it. You will want to avoid any criticism, judgment or advice-offering at this stage, but you will definitely want to communicate with other pain management team members and note your patient's present ways of dealing with their pain in the electronic health record even if you believe you must write in the electronic health record that it is "against medical advice." The intention in treatment will be to help your patient move from a pre-contemplative stage to a contemplative stage of change. This process can take some time and a few sessions with your patient and/or with their caretaker or family members.

Once your patient is in the contemplative stage of change, you will want to help them move to the preparation stage of change by asking them to weigh all the advantages and disadvantages of continuing to use certain maladaptive or ineffective strategies to deal with their chronic pain. Another task will be helping your patient mourn the loss of how they were before their chronic pain existed. The intention is to help your patient accept that they may always have chronic pain.

Once your patient enters the preparation stage of change, you will want to help the patient reframe their perception of chronic pain as a challenge rather than as a catastrophe. Once the patient is able to accept this reframe, you can help him or her establish realistic, specific, attainable goals, with a major goal being to develop and implement strategies to reduce their negative pain scale ratings while improving their positive ones over time. If your patient tends to be a perfectionist, and has high self-standards, it will be critical to help them lower their standards a bit by breaking large goals into sub-goals.

Once your patient is committed to an action plan, they can act on it to achieve their goals. You can then help your patient self-monitor how they are doing by asking them to assess their subjective ratings on each of the given pain scales at least once weekly. Your patient would then enter the maintenance phase of change by setting up periodic visits with you to evaluate how they are doing in changing their pain scale ratings. Your patient will also discuss specific triggers that can change their pain scale ratings in such a way as to increase, rather than reduce, their chronic pain.

There are many ways your patients can reduce their chronic pain. Here are some starter ideas they might try while collaborating with other pain management team members and auxiliary team members, to see what works best for them.

Medical "Starter Ideas"

- Trigger point injections, nerve blocks, epidural steroid and facet injections, nerve blocks, neural ablation (nerve burning), implantable pumps
- Use of an external transcutaneous electronic nerve stimulator (*TENS device*)
- Insertion of a more sophisticated TENS unit under the skin with electrodes placed at different locations.

Medications

Nonsteroidal Anti-Inflammatory Drugs (NSAIDs)
Aspirin (*Bayer*), Ibuprofen (*Motrin*), Naproxen (*Aleve*)

Analgesics
Acetaminophen (*Tylenol*)

Selective Serotonin Reuptake Inhibitors (SSRIs)
Citalopram (*Celexa*), Escitalopram (*Lexapro*), Fluoxetine (*Prozac*), Fluvoxamine (*Luvox*), Paroxetine (*Paxil*), Sertraline (*Zoloft*)

Selective Serotonin and Norepinephrine Reuptake Inhibitors (SSNRIs)
Venlafaxine (*Effexor*), Duloxetine (*Cymbalta*)

Tricyclic Antidepressants (TCAs)
Amitriptyline (*Elavil*), Imipramine (*Tofranil*), Clomipramine (*Anafranil*), Doxepin (*Sinequan*), Nortriptyline (*Pamelor*), Desipramine (*Nopramin*)

Anti-Convulsants (Anti-Epileptic Drugs)
Gabapentin (*Neurontin*), Carbamazepine (*Tegretol*), Pregabalin (*Lyrica*)

Opioids
Buprenorphine (*Suboxone*), Methadone, Hydrocodone (*Zohydro ER*), Oxycontin, Oxycodone (*OxyContin, Roxicodone*), Hydromorphone (*Dilaudid, Exalgo*), Morphine (*Avinza, Kadian, MSIR, MS Contin*), Oxymorphone Hydrochloride (*Opana*)

Muscle Relaxants
Baclofen, Chlorzoxazone (*Lorzone, Parafon Forte DSC*), Carisoprodol (*Soma*), Cyclobenzaprine (*e.g. Amrix, Cyclobenzaprine Comfort Pac, Fexmid, FlexePax, Flexeril, FusePaq Tabradol, Therabenzaprine-60*) Dantrolene (*Dantrium*), Diazepam (*Valium*), Metaxalone (*Skelaxin, Metaxall*), Methocarbamol (*Robaxin, Robaxin-750*), Tizanidine (*Comfort Pac with Tizanidine, Zanaflex, Zanaflex capsule*)

Topical Agents
Amitriptyline, Xylocaine, Lignocaine (*Lidocaine*), Ketamine, DMSO, Capsaicin

Medical Marijuana

Surgery

Physical Therapy

Chiropractic Treatment

Orthotics

Hot or Cold Compresses

Stretching

Exercise

Nutrition for weight loss and maintenance

Aquatic Therapy

Probiotics

On your mark, ready, set.....

Other "Starter Ideas"

Education
(courses, seminars, workshops, webinars, CDs, DVDs, podcasts, blogs)

Assertiveness Training

Promoting Happiness Skills

Anger Management

Diaphragmatic Breathing

Progressive Muscle Relaxation

Work with a Trainer

Yoga

Tai Chi

Massage

Hypnosis

Biofeedback

Acupuncture

Herbology

Stress Management

Meditation
(mindfulness, prayer, the relaxation response, visual imagery)

Cognitive Therapy

Behavior Therapy

Distraction

Socialization
(connectedness, blogs, websites, support groups)

"Bibliotherapy"
(using self-help workbooks)

Art or Music Therapy

Journaling

Gardening

Humor

Dramatics

Pet Therapy

Light Therapy

Aroma Therapy

Sound Therapy

Reiki

Reflexology

Igor patiently stood by to throw the pain switch.

Chapter 5: The Five Pain Scales

Once your patient decides to try some of their starter ideas (like those listed in Chapter 4), it is essential that they monitor how these activities and strategies impact their pain levels. To do this, your patient needs to rate themselves on the five pain scales at least once weekly. Remember that pain is subjective and includes not just your patient's physical pain, but their life stress, their emotional pain, their pain from negative thinking and from their lack of fortitude.

Your patient is familiar with the standard medical question, "What is your level of physical pain on a scale from 1 to 10 (with 1 to 4 being minimal pain and 7 to 10 being severe pain)?" They can rate their level of pain weekly in this same "level of pain from 1 to 10" way for all the scales. Most of the scales (except for the Fortitude Scale) identify higher ratings of 7 to 10 as not being in a healthy range. The opposite is true for the Fortitude Scale and the "Happiness" item on the Emotional Pain Scale, where the higher your patient's rating on these scale items, the better your patient is doing in fighting their pain.

Over time, your patient will want to use strategies to lower their pain levels to a range of 1 to 4 on most of the scale items. On the Happiness item on the Emotional Pain Scale and on all of the items on the Fortitude Scale, your patient will want to improve their levels to land between 7 to 10.

Using the pain scales will help your patient remain in the maintenance stage of change and empower them to self-monitor in an ongoing manner so as to prevent relapses. If your patient finds that certain strategies are not working, they can always choose others that may be more helpful in reducing their pain levels.

In Chapters 7 through 12, I provide you with specific ways to help improve your patient's scale ratings over time. In this chapter, however, let's take a closer look at each of the five pain scales.

The Physical Pain Scale

The Physical Pain Scale is most similar to the standard, subjective rating scale you presently use and which is required in electronic health records to address how your patient experiences pain. The revised scale featured in this book identifies how daily experiences impact your patient's pain severity by the hour and by period of the day. To use this scale, your patient will first keep a pain diary by rating their pain experiences on a scale of 1-10 (with 1 being least painful, 10 being most painful) at each hour for one day, then for three periods of the day for at least two days in one week. The different ratings help identify the activities your patient is involved in during each rating period, and the location and severity of your patient's pain, using a multitude of different adjectives describing pain sensations. A full week of ratings can help you and your patient determine certain patterns, like situations that led your patient to feel varying levels of pain at certain times of the day. Doing this al-

"Not too bad, except that my heart aches, and a drowsy
numbness pains my senses, feel light-headed,..."

by J.B. Handelsman

PHYSICAL PAIN SCALE (1 DAY)

NAME: Jane   DATE: 5/24

Please rate your physical pain during a day, per hour, on a scale from 1-10. Please describe what you are doing, the location of the pain, whether it is constant or comes and goes, and what the pain is like using the adjectives on the next page.

TIME: 7:00 AM

1	2	3	4	5	6	(7)	8	9	10
Low Pain					Moderate Pain				Intense Pain

Early morning getting up from bed. Pain is in different joints especially right hip aching, agonizing, stiff

TIME: 8 am

1	2	3	4	(5)	6	7	8	9	10
Low Pain				Moderate Pain				Intense Pain	

Having breakfast, sitting watching news. Aching all over comes + goes, aching, stiff, nagging

TIME: 9 am

1	2	3	(4)	5	6	7	8	9	10
Low Pain					Moderate Pain				Intense Pain

I am going to work — joints — upper joints comes + goes, sore — tender — warm

TIME: 10 am

1	2	3	4	5	6	7	8	(9)	10
Low Pain					Moderate Pain				Intense Pain

Walking from desk through office, Constant multiple joints Pulsing agonizing, sharp

TIME: 11 am

1	2	3	4	(5)	6	7	8	9	10
Low Pain				Moderate Pain				Intense Pain	

Sitting at desk - office work, Shoulders, elbows + wrists on both arms. Constant excrutiating, distressi radiating.

TIME: _12 pm_   1   2   3   4   5   6   7   (8)   9   10
Low Pain   Moderate Pain   Intense Pain

Walking to lunch. Pain comes + goes radiates to
legs. Pins and needles, tingling, stinging

TIME: _1:00 pm_   1   2   3   (4)   5   6   7   8   9   10
Low Pain   Moderate Pain   Intense Pain

at desk taking 5 minutes to relax. Pain all over body.
Constant, mild, cool, tender.

TIME: _2:00 pm_   1   2   3   4   5   6   7   8   (9)   10
Low Pain   Moderate Pain   Intense Pain

Hurts working at desk, upper multiple joints
Constant, agonizing, sore, distressing.

Some words that can help you describe the way your pain feels. Is it ____

Aching? ✓	Cramping?	Taut?	Crippling?	Gnawing?
Freezing?	Unbearable?	Heavy?	Hot or burning?	Nagging? ✓
Numb?	Sharp? ✓	Shooting? ✓	Squeezing?	Cold?
Sickening? ✓	Splitting?	Tight? ✓	Dreadful?	Stabbing? ✓
Punishing or cruel? ✓	Cool? ✓	Bolts?	Tender? ✓	Throbbing?
Agonizing?	Excruciating? ✓	Tiring? ✓	Distressing? ✓	Stiffness? ✓
Pulling?	Flickering?	Pricking?	Pinching?	Vicious?
Mild? ✓	Intense?	Pulsing?	Intermittent?	Scalding?
Exhausting?	Sore? ✓	Wretched?	Terrifying?	Killing?
Beating?	Jumping?	Miserable?	Piercing?	Drilling?
Cutting?	Tearing?	Nauseating?	Constant?	Stinging?
Electrical?	Pounding?	Tugging?	Penetrating?	Knot-like?
Horrible? ✓	Smarting?	Pins/Needles? ✓	Radiating? ✓	Varying?
Rasping?	Annoying? ✓	Quivering?	Itchy?	Suffocating?
Spreading?	Dull?	Tingling? ✓	Grueling?	Drawing?

63

PHYSICAL PAIN SCALE (2 DAY)

Please rate your physical pain for **2 days during the morning, afternoon and evening** on a scale from 1-10. Please describe what you are doing, the location of the pain, whether it is constant, or comes and goes, and what the pain is like using the adjectives on the next page.

DATE: 5/25

Morning   Time: 8am

1	2	3	4	5	6	⑦	8	9	10
Low Pain				Moderate Pain				Intense Pain	

Having breakfast reading newspaper. Aching all over joints - constant-distressing, agonizing + sore

Afternoon   Time: 2:00 pm

1	2	3	4	5	6	7	8	⑨	10
Low Pain				Moderate Pain				Intense Pain	

At work desk multiple joint pain Comes + goes radiating, pins + needles, stinging

Evening   Time: 7:00 pm

1	2	3	4	5	6	7	⑧	9	10
Low Pain				Moderate Pain				Intense Pain	

Laying down in bed watching TV. Multiple joints especially arm+back +neck, aching, pulsating + pinchin

DATE: 5/26

Morning   Time: 7:00 am

1	2	3	④	5	6	7	8	9	10
Low Pain				Moderate Pain				Intense Pain	

Getting dressed, ate, multiple joints Constant sore, agonizing distressing

Afternoon   Time: _1:00 pm_

1   2   3   (4)   5   6   7   8   9   10
Low Pain   Moderate Pain   Intense Pain

Back from lunch, Pain comes + goes, Mostly neck +
arms. Tender, sore + aching

Evening   Time: _9:00 pm_

1   2   3   (4)   5   6   7   8   9   10
Low Pain   Moderate Pain   Intense Pain

Laying down reading. Comes + goes
       Tiring, tender + dull

Some words that can help you describe the way your pain feels. Is it ____

Aching? ✓   Cramping?   Taut?'   Crippling?   Gnawing?
Freezing?   Unbearable?   Heavy?   Hot or burning?   Nagging?
Numb?   Sharp?   Shooting?   Squeezing?   Cold?
Sickening?   Splitting?   Tight?   Dreadful?   Stabbing?
Punishing or cruel? Cool?   Bolts?   Tender? ✓   Throbbing?
Agonizing? ✓   Excruciating?   Tiring? ✓   Distressing? ✓   Stiffness?
Pulling?   Flickering?   Pricking?   Pinching? ✓   Vicious?
Mild?   Intense?   Pulsing? ✓   Intermittent?   Scalding?
Exhausting?   Sore? ✓   Wretched?   Terrifying?   Killing?
Beating?   Jumping?   Miserable?   Piercing?   Drilling?
Cutting?   Tearing?   Nauseating?   Constant? ✓   Stinging? ✓
Electrical?   Pounding?   Tugging?   Penetrating?   Knot-like?
Horrible?   Smarting?   Pins/Needles? ✓   Radiating? ✓   Varying?
Rasping?   Annoying?   Quivering?   Itchy?   Suffocating?
Spreading?   Dull? ✓   Tingling?   Grueling?   Drawing?

lows your patient to generate specific strategies to reduce their pain levels.

The patient completing the two sample Physical Pain Rating Scales is Jane, a 46-year-old single female who has a history of having fibromyalgia. She has complained bitterly of having chronic pain for many years, having at least 11 tender points that are sensitive throughout her body. She has chronic fatigue, memory problems, and feels like she has constant "brain fog" from difficulty with her thinking. She experiences depression and anxiety, and has low self-esteem, poor coping skills, and frequent panic attacks. She has settled for a lower-paying job as a day care provider where she has difficulty picking up toddlers and loses her patience easily.

A review of Jane's physical health scales indicates that she has less pain in the morning, except for overall stiffness upon getting up from bed. Her pain subsides when she is doing self-care activities like having breakfast and being distracted from pain signals by watching the news. The pain remains low while she's driving to work but increases substantially when she walks around the day care facility performing child care responsibilities. Jane's pain lowers substantially when she takes a break to sit at her desk, then increases substantially when she walks around the day care facility, and even when she goes to lunch, and then when she has to stand or do chores while caring for the toddlers. Taking a five-minute break to meditate at her desk brings some relief but it is not long-lasting, as her pain increases when she performs more demanding job tasks. Her pain subsides only when she can lie down to relax from feeling chronically fatigued.

Jane's pain fluctuates between being constant and coming and going throughout the day. She has multiple pain sites that are indicative of fibromyalgia. It's difficult to read her descriptions of the tormenting pain she feels. Clearly, she is suffering immensely from daily work tasks.

Judging from just her physical pain ratings, Jane would do best if you recommend that she obtain a quieter, less physically taxing desk job where she can take frequent breaks while doing simpler, non-physical tasks. The distraction of doing easy tasks would be helpful for her, as would working in a quieter, more supportive environment.

It would be helpful for you to know if Jane experiences more or less pain based on doing tasks that require different postures, like bending forwards (flexion) or backwards (extension). Also, you may want to clarify with Jane how long she can maintain the strength to walk without pain. You may want to recommend a further evaluation by a physiatrist, physical therapist or chiropractor (if you are not one of these healthcare providers) to help determine what types of tasks would be easier for Jane to perform than the ones she presently does.

Try having your chronic pain patient keep a record of their physical pain ratings for a period of at least three days during a week, using the sample forms on the next pages. Then use the questions below to help them identify patterns of pain or insights about their pain.

- Where is their pain? Do they notice any particular patterns in their pain levels during the day?
- When are their physical pain levels lowest and when are they highest?
- What situations or activities reduce their pain and what activities aggravate it?
- Do they experience more or less pain from flexing their body than extending it? Are they lifting from their hips or while bending over (thus putting excessive weight on their back)?

Based on their responses, can you think of any ways they can reduce their physical pain levels on these scales?

PHYSICAL PAIN SCALE (1 DAY)

NAME: _____   DATE: _____

    Please rate your physical pain during a day, per hour, on a scale from 1-10. Please describe what you are doing, the location of the pain, whether it is constant or comes and goes, and what the pain is like using the adjectives on the next page.

TIME: _____   1   2   3   4   5   6   7   8   9   10

                        Low Pain   Moderate Pain   Intense Pain

_____

_____

TIME: _____   1   2   3   4   5   6   7   8   9   10

                        Low Pain   Moderate Pain   Intense Pain

_____

_____

TIME: _____   1   2   3   4   5   6   7   8   9   10

                        Low Pain   Moderate Pain   Intense Pain

_____

_____

TIME: _____   1   2   3   4   5   6   7   8   9   10

                        Low Pain   Moderate Pain   Intense Pain

_____

_____

TIME: _____   1   2   3   4   5   6   7   8   9   10

                        Low Pain   Moderate Pain   Intense Pain

_____

_____

TIME: _____ 1 2 3 4 5 6 7 8 9 10
Low Pain   Moderate Pain   Intense Pain

_____

_____

TIME: _____ 1 2 3 4 5 6 7 8 9 10
Low Pain   Moderate Pain   Intense Pain

_____

_____

TIME: _____ 1 2 3 4 5 6 7 8 9 10
Low Pain   Moderate Pain   Intense Pain

_____

_____

Some words that can help you describe the way your pain feels. Is it ____

Aching?	Cramping?	Taut?	Crippling?	Gnawing?
Freezing?	Unbearable?	Heavy?	Hot or burning?	Nagging?
Numb?	Sharp?	Shooting?	Squeezing?	Cold?
Sickening?	Splitting?	Tight?	Dreadful?	Stabbing?
Punishing or cruel?	Cool?	Bolts?	Tender?	Throbbing?
Agonizing?	Excruciating?	Tiring?	Distressing?	Stiffness?
Pulling?	Flickering?	Pricking?	Pinching?	Vicious?
Mild?	Intense?	Pulsing?	Intermittent?	Scalding?
Exhausting?	Sore?	Wretched?	Terrifying?	Killing?
Beating?	Jumping?	Miserable?	Piercing?	Drilling?
Cutting?	Tearing?	Nauseating?	Constant?	Stinging?
Electrical?	Pounding?	Tugging?	Penetrating?	Knot-like?
Horrible?	Smarting?	Pins/Needles?	Radiating?	Varying?
Rasping?	Annoying?	Quivering?	Itchy?	Suffocating?
Spreading?	Dull?	Tingling?	Grueling?	Drawing?

PHYSICAL PAIN SCALE (2 DAY)

Please rate your physical pain for **2 days during the morning, afternoon and evening** on a scale from 1-10. Please describe what you are doing, the location of the pain, whether it is constant, or comes and goes, and what the pain is like using the adjectives on the next page.

DATE: _____

Morning   **Time:** _____

1	2	3	4	5	6	7	8	9	10
Low Pain				Moderate Pain					Intense Pain

_____

_____

Afternoon   **Time:** _____

1	2	3	4	5	6	7	8	9	10
Low Pain				Moderate Pain					Intense Pain

_____

_____

Evening   **Time:** _____

1	2	3	4	5	6	7	8	9	10
Low Pain				Moderate Pain					Intense Pain

_____

_____

DATE: _____

Morning   **Time:** _____

1	2	3	4	5	6	7	8	9	10
Low Pain				Moderate Pain					Intense Pain

_____

_____

Afternoon   **Time:** _____

$\quad$ 1 $\quad$ 2 $\quad$ 3 $\quad$ 4 $\quad$ 5 $\quad$ 6 $\quad$ 7 $\quad$ 8 $\quad$ 9 $\quad$ 10
$\quad$ Low Pain $\qquad\qquad$ Moderate Pain $\qquad\qquad$ Intense Pain

_____

_____

Evening   **Time:** _____

$\quad$ 1 $\quad$ 2 $\quad$ 3 $\quad$ 4 $\quad$ 5 $\quad$ 6 $\quad$ 7 $\quad$ 8 $\quad$ 9 $\quad$ 10
$\quad$ Low Pain $\qquad\qquad$ Moderate Pain $\qquad\qquad$ Intense Pain

_____

_____

Some words that can help you describe the way your pain feels. Is it ____

Aching?	Cramping?	Taut?	Crippling?	Gnawing?
Freezing?	Unbearable?	Heavy?	Hot or burning?	Nagging?
Numb?	Sharp?	Shooting?	Squeezing?	Cold?
Sickening?	Splitting?	Tight?	Dreadful?	Stabbing?
Punishing or cruel?	Cool?	Bolts?	Tender?	Throbbing?
Agonizing?	Excruciating?	Tiring?	Distressing?	Stiffness?
Pulling?	Flickering?	Pricking?	Pinching?	Vicious?
Mild?	Intense?	Pulsing?	Intermittent?	Scalding?
Exhausting?	Sore?	Wretched?	Terrifying?	Killing?
Beating?	Jumping?	Miserable?	Piercing?	Drilling?
Cutting?	Tearing?	Nauseating?	Constant?	Stinging?
Electrical?	Pounding?	Tugging?	Penetrating?	Knot-like?
Horrible?	Smarting?	Pins/Needles?	Radiating?	Varying?
Rasping?	Annoying?	Quivering?	Itchy?	Suffocating?
Spreading?	Dull?	Tingling?	Grueling?	Drawing?

The Life Stress Pain Scale

Your patient's ratings on the Life Stress Pain Scale identify the level of stress they experience for those applicable items that impact their pain levels. Counting only those items that are rated between 7 and 10, your patient then adds them up and divides them by the number of items counted to determine their overall level of present life stress. Then they rate subjectively the impact of that level of life stress on their family life, work, and social functioning. As with the Physical Pain Scale, your patient's ratings are based on subjective ratings from 1 (low) to 10 (high).

It is helpful for your patient to have a significant other in their life help them rate items on their Life Stress Pain Scale. That's because another person's perception and perspective can reduce the potential for your patient to minimize or magnify each life stress they are experiencing.

The patient completing the Life Stress Pain Scale shown in the example here is Jim, a 55-year-old married salesman who experienced a major heart attack a few years ago that ultimately led to quadruple bypass surgery. The high rating he assigned to medical illness as a stressor was not surprising, nor were his high ratings of surgeries and aging. He rated job loss high, given that his history was one of attaining high-salaried, secure positions, then quickly becoming disenchanted with them because he never thought each one was good enough. He gave marital discord a high rating due to his wife being upset that he remained overweight, didn't exercise and was away often each week. Note that his average rating of 4 for major life stressors between 7 and 10 was mathematically incorrect and well below Jim's actual average of 8.6. Even his low, subjective rating of 3 of the impact of major life stress on his family life, work, and social life didn't seem to make sense. This may have resulted from Jim's tendency to minimize and deny, and to usually hold everyone else responsible for his life difficulties. He only sought help for his pain because his wife suggested he do so.

Jim may need help first in becoming educated about how life stressors can impact chronic pain. If he continues to minimize the importance of life stressors because he is in a pre-contemplative stage of change, then it may be best for you to ask him if significant others are concerned about how he is coping with life stressors and why they are so concerned. It may be further helpful to simply empathize and be nonjudgmental with Jim while reviewing with him the possible short- and long-term consequences of minimizing the impact of his stressors.

LIFE STRESS PAIN SCALE

Please review your present experiences of stress below and rate on a scale of 1-10 the degree to which you believe each stressor impacts your pain. (1 is no impact, 10 is strong impact.)

If you have a significant other person in your life, please consider asking him/her to help you complete the ratings for this scale.

NAME: _Jim_   DATE: _June 28, 2017_

- ❑ Housing
- ❑ Engagement
- ❑ Pregnancy
- ❑ Teenagers
- ❑ In-laws
- ❑ Hobbies
- ❑ Single
- *10* ❑ Hours at Work
- ❑ Finances
- ❑ Rape
- ❑ Natural Catastrophe
- ❑ Caring for Elder(s)
- ❑ Legal Issues
- ❑ Insurance Concerns
- ❑ Workman's Compensation
- ❑ Experiencing/ Witnessing/Hearing About Trama
- ❑ Education

- ❑ Relationships
- ❑ Childbirth
- ❑ Parents
- ❑ Friendships
- ❑ Affair(s)
- ❑ Post-Marital Conflict
- ❑ Increased Work Responsibilities
- ❑ Wills/Estates
- ❑ Death of Loved One
- ❑ Lack of Assertiveness
- ❑ Substance Use/ Abuse/Dependence
- *9* ❑ Medical Issues
- ❑ Getting/ Not Getting Disability Insurance
- ❑ Retirement
- ❑ Isolation

- ❑ Marital Problems
- ❑ Children's Illness
- ❑ Role Functions
- ❑ Social Life
- ❑ Separation
- ❑ Single Parenting
- ❑ Multi-Tasking Demands
- *6* ❑ Aging
- ❑ Grandparenting
- ❑ Religious Affiliation
- ❑ Other Addictions (Phone, Internet, Gambling, Porn)
- *9* ❑ Hospitalization(s)
- ❑ Listening to or Watching News
- ❑ Dating
- ❑ Infertility
- ❑ Raising Children

- ❑ Siblings
- ❑ Lack of Exercise
- ❑ Divorce
- ❑ Balancing Parenting and work
- ❑ Career Issues/ Dissatisfaction
- ❑ War
- ❑ Unemployment
- ❑ Verbal or Physical Abuse
- ❑ Getting into an Accident (with/without) injuries
- *10* ❑ Surgery(ies)
- ❑ Politics
- ❑ Other:
- _____
- _____
- _____

Please indicate the average rating of your present stressors between 7 and 10 that impact your pain. Add up only items rated from 7 to 10 and divide the total by the number of items counted to find your average rating.

| 1 | 2 | 3 | (4) | 5 | 6 | 7 | 8 | 9 | 10 |

Not a problem   Somewhat of a problem   A very large problem

Next, rate the impact of that level of life stress on your

Family (1-10)	**Work** (1-10)	**Social Life** (1-10)
3	3	3

73

On the Life Stress Pain Scale, have your patient rate their level of pain from each major life stressor event that they've identified as rating between 7 and 10. Then have them calculate their average rating. Finally, ask them what they think is the subjective impact of their average life stress level on their family life, work (if they are employed) and social life.

Looking at their answers on the Life Stress Pain Scale, ask them these questions:

- Does your patient know which life stressors impact their pain levels the most?
- Do they notice how the average rating of life stressors impacts the areas of family life, work, and social life?
- Judging from this scale, can you help your patient to think of ways to reduce any of their major life stressors?

The pressures of life were squeezing the life out of Mort.

LIFE STRESS PAIN SCALE

Please review your present experiences of stress below and rate on a scale of 1-10 the degree to which you believe each stressor impacts your pain. (1 is no impact, 10 is strong impact.)

If you have a significant other person in your life, please consider asking him/her to help you complete the ratings for this scale.

NAME: _____   DATE: _____

- ❏ Housing
- ❏ Engagement
- ❏ Pregnancy
- ❏ Teenagers
- ❏ In-laws
- ❏ Hobbies
- ❏ Single
- ❏ Hours at Work
- ❏ Finances
- ❏ Rape
- ❏ Natural Catastrophe
- ❏ Caring for Elder(s)
- ❏ Legal Issues
- ❏ Insurance Concerns
- ❏ Workman's Compensation
- ❏ Experiencing/ Witnessing/Hearing About Trama
- ❏ Education

- ❏ Relationships
- ❏ Childbirth
- ❏ Parents
- ❏ Friendships
- ❏ Affair(s)
- ❏ Post-Marital Conflict
- ❏ Increased Work Responsibilities
- ❏ Wills/Estates
- ❏ Death of Loved One
- ❏ Lack of Assertiveness
- ❏ Substance Use/ Abuse/Dependence
- ❏ Medical Issues
- ❏ Getting/ Not Getting Disability Insurance
- ❏ Retirement
- ❏ Isolation

- ❏ Marital Problems
- ❏ Children's Illness
- ❏ Role Functions
- ❏ Social Life
- ❏ Separation
- ❏ Single Parenting
- ❏ Multi-Tasking Demands
- ❏ Aging
- ❏ Grandparenting
- ❏ Religious Affiliation
- ❏ Other Addictions (Phone, Internet, Gambling, Porn)
- ❏ Hospitalization(s)
- ❏ Listening to or Watching News
- ❏ Dating
- ❏ Infertility
- ❏ Raising Children

- ❏ Siblings
- ❏ Lack of Exercise
- ❏ Divorce
- ❏ Balancing Parenting and work
- ❏ Career Issues/ Dissatisfaction
- ❏ War
- ❏ Unemployment
- ❏ Verbal or Physical Abuse
- ❏ Getting into an Accident (with/without) injuries
- ❏ Surgery(ies)
- ❏ Politics
- ❏ Other:
- _____
- _____
- _____

Please indicate the average rating of your present stressors between 7 and 10 that impact your pain. Add up only items rated from 7 to 10 and divide the total by the number of items counted to find your average rating.

1	2	3	4	5	6	7	8	9	10
Not a problem				Somewhat of a problem			A very large problem		

Next, rate the impact of that level of life stress on your

Family (1-10)	Work (1-10)	Social Life (1-10)

The Emotional Pain Scale

Your patient's ratings on the Emotional Pain Scale are simpler than those on the Physical and Life Stress Pain Scales. You would like to know your patient's subjective perception of how depressed, anxious, angry and unhappy they think they are. Pain may be inferred from their having high ratings (ranging from 7 to 10) on depression, anxiety or anger. In contrast, their high rating for happiness would suggest that they feel quite content at this time despite having pain.

As with the Life Stress Pain Scale, it would be helpful for a significant other in your patient's life to help them rate their four emotional states. Having someone else who knows your patient's present emotional condition can help improve the validity and reliability of their ratings.

Example of the Emotional Pain Scale

The patient completing the sample Emotional Pain Scale is Vivian, a 63-year-old widow who suffers from severe osteoarthritis in her hips and shoulders. She has been in pain clinics multiple times for trigger point injections and for an ongoing prescription of Tramadol, an opiate that gave her moderate pain relief but her healthcare provider will no longer prescribe because of tightening federal and state regulations. Vivian is not considered a candidate for a full hip replacement surgery given that her X-rays showed only moderate osteoarthritis and bone-to-bone condition.

When you look at Vivian's responses on the Emotional Pain Scale, it is clear that her emotional states have a significant impact on her pain ratings. She is severely depressed and lonely, although not actively suicidal, but does admit to having frequent suicidal ideation and feelings of isolation. Her adult children refuse to be with her because of her frequent complaining and the multitude of angry outbursts she has when interacting with them. Her high anxiety rating is realistic and indicative of her emotional instability and scant motivation to work. Vivian relies only on disability payments for income. She experiences excruciating pain levels and is often at risk for suicide.

Vivian needs much support in dealing with all of her emotional conditions. She may benefit from one or several medications to help reduce her osteoarthritic condition, depression and anxiety. If necessary, she may need to be referred to a rheumatologist for a second opinion. Vivian can benefit from supportive therapy to help her cope and develop further resilience skills including managing her anger. A family intervention might help ease the disconnect between Vivian and her children, and help her develop support networks beyond them.

EMOTIONAL PAIN SCALE

NAME: **Vivian**   DATE: **6/28/17**

Please review your present experiences of the emotional conditions noted below and rate on a scale of 1 – 10 the degree to which you believe each one has an impact on your level of pain.

If you have a significant other person in your life please consider asking him/her to help you rate this scale.
(1 = I do not believe this to be true) to (10 = I do believe this to be true)

(Note: Happiness Scale is scored differently than the other three scales - the higher the score, the better the rating)

1. DEPRESSION:

1	2	3	4	5	6	7	8	9	10

Low **Moderate** **Severe**
(low-sad-hurt) (unhappy-aggrieved-dejected) (depressed-miserable-despondent)

2. ANXIETY:

1	2	3	4	5	6	7	8	9	10

Low **Moderate** **Severe**
(concerned-uncomfortable-bothered) (worried-upset-troubled) (frightened-overwhelmed-panicky)

3. ANGER:

1	2	3	4	5	6	7	8	9	10

Low **Moderate** **Severe**
(annoyed-hurt-disappointed) (frustrated-upset-mad) (furious-enraged-incensed)

4. HAPPINESS:

1	2	3	4	5	6	7	8	9	10

Low **Moderate** **Severe**
(glad-comfortable-content) (cheerful-pleased-happy) (blissful-exhilarated-ecstatic)

- Judging from their scale ratings, how does your patient see themselves coping presently with each emotional state?
- What factors do they think are contributing to the impact of each emotional state on their experience of pain?
- What is the impact of each emotional state on their relationships with others?
- What can your patient do to reduce their negative emotional ratings and improve their happiness?

Stu, getting last-second instructions before jumping into the game.

EMOTIONAL PAIN SCALE

NAME: _____   DATE: _____

   Please review your present experiences of the emotional conditions noted below and rate on a scale of 1 – 10 the degree to which you believe each one has an impact on your level of pain.

   If you have a significant other person in your life please consider asking him/her to help you rate this scale.
   (1 = I do not believe this to be true) to (10 = I do believe this to be true)

   (Note: Happiness Scale is scored differently than the other three scales - the higher the score, the better the rating)

1. DEPRESSION:
1	2	3	4	5	6	7	8	9	10

          Low   **Moderate**   **Severe**

    (low-sad-hurt)   (unhappy-aggrieved-dejected)   (depressed-miserable-despondent)

2. ANXIETY:
1	2	3	4	5	6	7	8	9	10

          Low   **Moderate**   **Severe**

(concerned-uncomfortable-bothered)   (worried-upset-troubled)   (frightened-overwhelmed-panicky)

3. ANGER:
1	2	3	4	5	6	7	8	9	10

          Low   **Moderate**   **Severe**

 (annoyed-hurt-disappointed)   (frustrated-upset-mad)   (furious-enraged-incensed)

4. HAPPINESS:
1	2	3	4	5	6	7	8	9	10

          Low   **Moderate**   **Severe**

 (glad-comfortable-content)   (cheerful-pleased-happy)   (blissful-exhilarated-ecstatic)

The Cognitive Appraisal of Pain Scale

Your patient's ratings on the Cognitive Appraisal of Pain Scale verify the importance of their understanding the impact of their negative thinking, based on the works of Aaron Beck on cognitive therapy. Dr. Beck determined the relationship between how one thinks and how one feels. If a patient thinks negatively, they will have increased depression, anxiety or anger. If they think positively, they will feel happier and have less emotional "pain."

As your patient did on the Life Stress and Emotional Pain Scales, they should also enlist the help of a significant other to rate each negative thinking error, because your patient's thinking errors may not be so apparent to them.

Common "thinking errors"
around chronic pain include the following:

1. All-or-nothing (dichotomous) thinking. Your patient views most situations as falling into one of two categories (always versus never, perfect versus terrible). How often does your patient catch themselves making statements like these? "I can't work because I always have pain" or "I never feel good."

2. Over-generalization. Your patient reaches more global negative conclusions that go well beyond that one situation. Do thoughts like these sound familiar to your patient? "I can't do what I used to do because I can't bike" or "I won't be able to do anything anymore because I can't walk long distances."

3. Mental filtering. Your patient pays more attention to a single detail instead of seeing the whole picture. How often does your patient think this way? "My pain means that I'm inadequate" or "I couldn't go shopping today, so that means I'm not good enough."

4. Disqualifying the positive. Your patient tells themselves that their positive experiences don't count. How often does your patient think something like, "I was able to cook one meal last night but one night out of twenty doesn't mean much"?

5. Jumping to conclusions (futuristic thinking). Your patient focuses on the future and predicts it negatively without considering other possibilities. How often does your patient think something like this? "Oh no! Here comes the pain again. I'll definitely wind up in the emergency room" or "I know I'll feel a lot of pain tomorrow because it's going to rain."

6. Catastrophizing (magnification). Your patient exaggerates the importance of negative things and minimizes the positive, focusing on the worst-case scenario instead of the best-case scenario. Your patient makes a mountain out of a molehill. How often does your patient think of these types of thoughts? "My pain will be totally unbearable" or "I can't handle this anymore!"

7. Emotional reasoning. Your patient thinks that if they feel something so strongly, then it must be true. How often does your patient have negative thoughts like these? "I don't care what my physical therapist says! I feel that it can't be good for me." "I feel that it's going to be painful for me."

8. "Should" statements. Your patient holds fixed ideas as to how the world should, ought to, or must be true. (This may relate to your patient's high self-standards). Do these thoughts sound familiar to your patient? "I feel I should be able to walk five miles." "Everyone should understand why I can't exercise." "I have to take opioid pain medications."

9. Labeling. Your patient attaches a global, extreme negative label to themselves or to others. Does your patient often make judgments like these? "I'm stupid," or "I'm not good enough," or "All doctors are uncaring jerks."

10. Need for control. Your patient believes that they must control everything in their lives: themselves, their relationships, their emotions, or their personal situations. Does your patient find themselves having thoughts like these? "I need to know everything about what's going to happen." "The need to control helps me to not feel helpless and powerless."

11. Personalization. Your patient believes they are responsible for negative situations and that it is all their fault, even when there is no evidence to indicate that this is true. How often does your patient catch themselves thinking statements like these? "This pain is punishment for something I did wrong." "If I didn't have pain, then my spouse wouldn't be mad at me."

12. Underestimating personal strengths. Your patient minimizes the positive traits they have that can help them handle their pain. How often does your patient have these kinds of thoughts? "I can't handle my pain," or "It's not worth trying anymore."

13. Mind reading. Your patient thinks that the other person is having specific thoughts about them and their pain. How often does your patient have these types of thoughts? "My spouse thinks that I can't do anything because of my pain." Or, "My friend thinks that I am not doing enough to help myself."

How to Use the Cognitive Appraisal of Pain Scale to Determine How Much Your Patient's Thinking Can Make Them Feel Anxious or Depressed

The Cognitive Appraisal of Pain Scale can identify common patterns for your patients who suffer from heightened anxiety or depression. If your patient has a high anxiety level, they may score higher on certain cognitive appraisals than others. Of particular interest is your patient's rating on the control scale, since anxious people value security and have a difficult time feeling uncertain or helpless about situations. Your patient's "need for control" may be high if they are a perfectionist with high self-standards. The same is true for "should" statements because, if someone is highly anxious, they may invest a lot of energy in what they "should" be doing, but can't do, because they have chronic pain.

If your patient rates high on both Futuristic and Catastrophic Thinking, he or she is probably a person who worries constantly about a pessimistic future rather than being able to relax enough to enjoy each moment in time or consider the possibility of positive future outcomes. While future planning is a healthy skill, an overemphasis on the future can elicit obsessive thoughts and feelings of doubt and uncertainty that can parallel a higher-scaled score on the Need for Control scale.

Your patient may often perceive situations in all-or-nothing, black-and-white ways rather than taking into account the large grey area between extremes. Again, this is true if your patient is a perfectionist. Perhaps some of these statements sound familiar to your patients with chronic pain? "I'm either pain-free or in severe pain." "I have to be perfect or I'm inadequate." "I have to do exceedingly well or I'm terrible."

If your patient is very depressed, they may often disqualify the positive appraisal of a situation. It is easier for them to think their experiences will "always" be negative and "never" positive. They make overgeneralizations from one situation to every situation and may tend to filter in only negative conditions about it. They may make mountains out of molehills. Their future can seem catastrophic to them, without any appreciation for the positive possible outcomes, and they may have trouble reframing their future as an opportunity or challenge instead of a catastrophe. Patients who are depressed can be very hard on themselves. Perfectionists often become depressed if they can't meet high self-standards. If your patient personalizes or sees themselves at fault excessively, they may often blame themselves and feel over-responsible, even in situations for which responsibility should be attributed to others or over which they have no control.

Example of the Cognitive Appraisal of Pain Scale

The patient completing the sample scale is Wilson, a 45-year-old divorced man with a long history of chronic pain. He became severely depressed after being involved in a highly conflictual divorce that led to his estrangement from his three daughters, who perceived him as mentally unstable. His former wife disregarded how much pain Wilson had experienced from working so much, leaving little time for his family life. Wilson didn't exercise much, which led to his being overweight and having more pain.

Most of his ratings for negative cognitive appraisals are high, indicating extreme preoccupation with internal thoughts that render him extremely anxious and depressed. He is paralyzed by having so many thinking errors because he sits around most of the day, doing very little to distract himself except for working and watching TV.

When asked what he does to help his chronic pain, Wilson often gives all kinds of reasons for not doing anything. It is easy to see why he is so depressed and anxious. He relies excessively on obsessing, rather than considering the impact of his having so many high negative cognitive appraisals on his pain scale.

How might you help Wilson improve his situation? Given the extent of Wilson's high ratings on this scale, the best treatment would be to help him identify many activities that could distract him from being so focused on having so many negative thoughts. He could reduce both his anxiety and his depression by taking an interest in helping others, doing volunteer work or learning to play a musical instrument -- in short, doing anything that takes him outside of himself and his tendency to overthink.

COGNITIVE APPRAISAL OF PAIN SCALE

NAME: _Wilson_   DATE: _6/5/17_

Please rate these different cognitive appraisals on a scale of 1-10 to the degree to which you believe each appraisal to be true for you.

If you have a significant other person in your life please consider asking him/her to help you rate this scale.

(1 = I do not believe this to be true) to (10 = I do believe this to be true)

1. **ALL OR NOTHING (DICHOTOMOUS) THINKING:**

   You view most situations as falling into one of two distinct categories (always vs. never, perfect vs. terrible). How often do you catch yourself making statements like, "I can't work because I always have pain" or, "I never feel good"?

   1   2   3   4   5   6   7   (8)   9   10
   A little   Some   A Lot

2. **OVER GENERALIZATION:**

   You reach more global negative conclusions that go well beyond the one situation. How often do these kinds of thoughts sound familiar to you? "I can't do what I used to do because I can't bike" or, "I won't be able to do anything because I can't walk long distances."

   1   2   3   4   5   6   7   8   (9)   10
   A little   Some   A Lot

3. **MENTAL FILTERING:**

   You pay more attention to a single detail instead of seeing the whole picture. How often do you think something like, "My pain means that I'm inadequate" or, "I couldn't go shopping today means that I'm not good enough"?

   1   2   3   4   5   6   7   (8)   9   10
   A little   Some   A Lot

4. **DISQUALIFYING THE POSITIVE:**

   You tell yourself that positive experiences don't count. How often do you think something like, "I was able to cook one meal last night but one night out of twenty doesn't mean much"?

   1   2   3   4   5   6   7   (8)   9   10
   A little   Some   A Lot

5. **JUMPING TO CONCLUSIONS - FUTURISTIC THINKING:**

   You focus on the future and predict it negatively without considering other possibilities. How often do you think this kind of thought? "Oh no! Here comes the pain again. I'll definitely wind up in the emergency ward."

   1   2   3   4   5   6   7   8   (9)   10
   A little   Some   A Lot

6. **CATASTROPHIZING - MAGNIFICATION:**

   You exaggerate the importance of negative things and minimize the positive, focusing on the worst-case scenario versus the best-case scenario. You make a mountain out of a molehill. How often do you think of these kinds of thoughts? "My pain will be totally unbearable" or, "I can't handle this anymore!"

   1   2   3   4   5   6   7   8   (9)   10
   A little   Some   A Lot

Adapted by the author from materials by Aaron Beck, MD

7. EMOTIONAL REASONING:

You think that if you feel something so strongly, then it must be true. How often do you think these kinds of negative thoughts? "I don't care what my physical therapist says! I feel that it can't be good for me" or, "I feel that it's going to be painful."

1	2	3	4	5	6	7	(8)	9	10
A little				Some					A Lot

8. "SHOULD" STATEMENTS:

You hold fixed ideas as to how the world ought to, or must be true. (This may relate to high self-standards.) How often do you have thoughts like, "I should be able to walk 5 miles" or, "Everyone should understand why I can't exercise" or, "I have to take strong pain medications"?

1	2	3	4	5	6	7	(8)	9	10
A little				Some					A Lot

9. LABELING:

You attach a global, extreme negative label to yourself or others. How often do you catch yourself making judgments like these? "I'm stupid!" or, "I'm not good enough!" or, "All doctors are uncaring jerks!"

1	2	3	4	5	(6)	7	8	9	10
A little				Some					A Lot

10. NEED FOR CONTROL:

You believe that you must control everything in your life; yourself, your relationships, your emotions, or your personal situations. How often do you have thoughts like these? "I need to know everything about what's going to happen" or, "The need to control helps me to not feel helpless and powerless."

1	2	3	4	5	6	7	8	9	(10)
A little				Some					A Lot

11. PERSONALIZATION:

You believe you're responsible for negative situations and that it is all your fault, even when there is no evidence to indicate that this is true. How often do you catch yourself thinking statements like these? "This pain is punishment for something I did wrong" or, "If I don't have pain, then my spouse wouldn't be mad at me."

1	2	3	4	(5)	6	7	8	9	10
A little				Some					A Lot

12. UNDERESTIMATING YOUR STRENGTHS:

You minimize the positive traits that you have to handle your pain. How often do you have these kinds of thoughts? "I can't handle my pain" or, "It's not worth trying anymore."

1	2	3	4	5	6	7	8	(9)	10
A little				Some					A Lot

13. MIND READING:

You think that the other person is having specific thoughts about you and your pain. How often do you have these kinds of thoughts? "My spouse thinks that I can't do anything because of my pain" or, "My friend thinks that I'm not doing enough to help myself."

1	2	(3)	4	5	6	7	8	9	10
A little				Some					A Lot

Adapted by the author from materials by Aaron Beck, MD

Have
Your
Patient
Try It

As your patient fills out the Cognitive Appraisal of Pain Scale, have them rate the impact of each way of negative thinking on their pain levels. Have them enlist the help of a significant other to do this, if possible.

- Do they notice how any of the negative cognitive appraisals impact their pain?
- Do they notice any particular patterns?
- Can they come up with any rational responses to their high-rated negative ways of thinking when they catch themselves thinking or saying any of them?
- Do they notice any relationship between their pain level ratings on their Emotional Pain Scale and this one; in particular, their levels of anxiety or depression?

No matter how fast Sy ran, pain was catching up to him.

COGNITIVE APPRAISAL OF PAIN SCALE

NAME: _____   DATE: _____

Please rate these different cognitive appraisals on a scale of 1-10 to the degree to which you believe each appraisal to be true for you.

If you have a significant other person in your life please consider asking him/her to help you rate this scale.

(1 = I do not believe this to be true) to (10 = I do believe this to be true)

1. ALL OR NOTHING (DICHOTOMOUS) THINKING:

You view most situations as falling into one of two distinct categories (always vs. never, perfect vs. terrible). How often do you catch yourself making statements like, "I can't work because I always have pain" or, "I never feel good"?

1	2	3	4	5	6	7	8	9	10
A little				Some					A Lot

2. OVER GENERALIZATION:

You reach more global negative conclusions that go well beyond the one situation. How often do these kinds of thoughts sound familiar to you? "I can't do what I used to do because I can't bike" or, "I won't be able to do anything because I can't walk long distances."

1	2	3	4	5	6	7	8	9	10
A little				Some					A Lot

3. MENTAL FILTERING:

You pay more attention to a single detail instead of seeing the whole picture. How often do you think something like, "My pain means that I'm inadequate" or, "I couldn't go shopping today means that I'm not good enough"?

1	2	3	4	5	6	7	8	9	10
A little				Some					A Lot

4. DISQUALIFYING THE POSITIVE:

You tell yourself that positive experiences don't count. How often do you think something like, "I was able to cook one meal last night but one night out of twenty doesn't mean much"?

1	2	3	4	5	6	7	8	9	10
A little				Some					A Lot

5. JUMPING TO CONCLUSIONS - FUTURISTIC THINKING:

You focus on the future and predict it negatively without considering other possibilities. How often do you think this kind of thought? "Oh no! Here comes the pain again. I'll definitely wind up in the emergency ward."

1	2	3	4	5	6	7	8	9	10
A little				Some					A Lot

6. CATASTROPHIZING - MAGNIFICATION:

You exaggerate the importance of negative things and minimize the positive, focusing on the worst-case scenario versus the best-case scenario. You make a mountain out of a molehill. How often do you think of these kinds of thoughts? "My pain will be totally unbearable" or, "I can't handle this anymore!"

1	2	3	4	5	6	7	8	9	10
A little				Some					A Lot

7. EMOTIONAL REASONING:

You think that if you feel something so strongly, then it must be true. How often do you think these kinds of negative thoughts? "I don't care what my physical therapist says! I feel that it can't be good for me" or, "I feel that it's going to be painful."

1	2	3	4	5	6	7	8	9	10
A little				Some					A Lot

8. "SHOULD" STATEMENTS:

You hold fixed ideas as to how the world ought to, or must be true. (This may relate to high self-standards.) How often do you have thoughts like, "I should be able to walk 5 miles" or, "Everyone should understand why I can't exercise" or, "I have to take strong pain medications"?

1	2	3	4	5	6	7	8	9	10
A little				Some					A Lot

9. LABELING:

You attach a global, extreme negative label to yourself or others. How often do you catch yourself making judgments like these? "I'm stupid!" or, "I'm not good enough!" or, "All doctors are uncaring jerks!"

1	2	3	4	5	6	7	8	9	10
A little				Some					A Lot

10. NEED FOR CONTROL:

You believe that you must control everything in your life; yourself, your relationships, your emotions, or your personal situations. How often do you have thoughts like these? "I need to know everything about what's going to happen" or, "The need to control helps me to not feel helpless and powerless."

1	2	3	4	5	6	7	8	9	10
A little				Some					A Lot

11. PERSONALIZATION:

You believe you're responsible for negative situations and that it is all your fault, even when there is no evidence to indicate that this is true. How often do you catch yourself thinking statements like these? "This pain is punishment for something I did wrong" or, "If I don't have pain, then my spouse wouldn't be mad at me."

1	2	3	4	5	6	7	8	9	10
A little				Some					A Lot

12. UNDERESTIMATING YOUR STRENGTHS:

You minimize the positive traits that you have to handle your pain. How often do you have these kinds of thoughts? "I can't handle my pain" or, "It's not worth trying anymore."

1	2	3	4	5	6	7	8	9	10
A little				Some					A Lot

13. MIND READING:

You think that the other person is having specific thoughts about you and your pain. How often do you have these kinds of thoughts? "My spouse thinks that I can't do anything because of my pain" or, "My friend thinks that I'm not doing enough to help myself."

1	2	3	4	5	6	7	8	9	10
A little				Some					A Lot

Adapted by the author from materials by Aaron Beck, MD

The Fortitude Scale

Over the past few decades, there has been a major shift in the field of psychology towards emphasizing one's strengths. Professionals like Martin Seligman have conducted much research to indicate the positive impact of lessening "pain" by building positivity, optimism, happiness and resilience (the ability to bounce back from hardships or setbacks). Research has demonstrated that the critical factor that keeps people alive who are taken prisoner during wartime or are held hostage by terrorists is their sustaining hope. Building hope rests with a commitment to action and the ability to reframe pain as a challenge rather than a curse.

To take advantage of this research, I designed the Fortitude Scale to help your patients subjectively rate the personal strengths that could help them to reduce chronic pain. To do this, your patients must regain old or learn new coping skills and build their self-esteem by improving their level of self-care and self-efficacy. Increasing their resilience is just as important as learning to be assertive and think flexibly, to self-monitor well, and to problem-solve effectively. Who wouldn't find humor comforting, mindfulness meditation rewarding, and sustaining optimism helpful? Being grateful for what they have, however simple, is a necessity to contemplate on a daily basis, as is your patient's ability to love others no matter how severe their own experience of pain. Finally, there is "Emuna" or your patient's unconditional faith in G-d or a higher power.

The items listed on the Fortitude Scale are as follows:

1. Coping skills: *"You can handle it."*
2. Self-esteem: *"Feeling good about yourself."*
   A. Self-care: *"Take care of yourself."*
   B. Self-efficacy: *"Accomplish things."*
3. Assertiveness: *"Stand up for your rights."*
4. Exercise: *"Just do it."*
5. Distraction skills: *"Take the time to smell the roses."*
6. Mindfulness skills: *"Be here now."*
7. Problem-solving skills:
   "What is your problem?"
   "What are some of your plans?"
   "What is the best plan?"
   "Act on your plan."
   "How did you do?"
8. Self-monitoring skills: *"Think before you act."*
9. Cognitive flexibility skills: *"Go with the flow."*

10. Optimism skills: *"Hope for the future."*
11. Humor skills: *"Laugh and the world laughs with you."*
12. Resiliency skills: *"You can bounce back."*
13. Gratitude skills: *"Be thankful for what you have."*
14. Supportive system skills: *"Connect with family, friends and community."*
15. Loving skills: *"Do unto others as you would have them do unto you."*
16. Spirituality skills: *"Emuna -- one's unconditional faith in G-d"* (or a higher power).

Example of a Fortitude Scale

The patient completing the sample Fortitude Scale is Susan, a 32-year-old married woman who works full time in the medical profession. She often works overtime in high-stress situations. She shows fantastic strengths in many areas based on her Fortitude Scale ratings. For example, she has a balanced level of self-esteem between her self-care and self-efficacy, an excellent ability to assert herself when necessary, and a healthy ability to distract herself with activities like gardening, yoga, and playing the piano. Susan practices mindfulness meditation each morning and enjoys watching comedies rather than the news that is full of negativity. Of critical importance is her level of gratitude, her love for others and her passionate love for G-d, based on her religious upbringing.

Where she falls short is her ability to problem-solve and shift into doing new tasks when she is focusing on current ones. In addition, she needs help with building resilience (the ability to bounce back from hardships). Susan needs help in improving her brain's executive functions, particularly the sequence of problem-solving effectively including problem recognition, cause-and-effect reasoning, and self-monitoring skills. Helping her identify her values, interests, and abilities would prove useful, as would reflecting on how she was able to bounce back from former upsets. Of particular concern would be helping her recognize the positive impact of her high Fortitude Scale ratings and using these skills to reduce her chronic pain.

You can leap over the forces of pain.

FORTITUDE SCALE

NAME: Susan

DATE: 6/26/17

Please review your present experiences of the conditions noted below and rate on a scale of 1 – 10 the degree to which you believe each condition has an impact on your level of pain.

Note: The higher the rating, the stronger the belief.

If you have a significant other person in your life, please consider asking him/her to help you rate this scale.
(1 = I do not believe this to be true) to (10 = I do believe this to be true)

1. **COPING SKILLS:** "You can handle it"

   1   2   3   (4)   5   6   7   8   9   10
   Low   Moderate   High

2. **SELF-ESTEEM:** "Feel good about yourself"
   Balance between

   A. SELF-CARE SKILLS "Take care of yourself"

   1   2   3   4   (5)   6   7   8   9   10
   Low   Moderate   High

   And B. SELF-EFFICACY SKILLS "Accomplish things

   1   2   3   4   (5)   6   7   8   9   10
   Low   Moderate   High

3. **ASSERTIVENESS SKILLS:** "Stand up for your rights"

   1   2   3   4   5   6   7   8   (9)   10
   Low   Moderate   High

4. **EXERCISE SKILLS:** "Just do it!"

   1   2   3   (4)   5   6   7   8   9   10
   Low   Moderate   High

5. **DISTRACTION SKILLS:** "Take the time to smell the roses"

   1   2   3   4   5   6   (7)   8   9   10
   Low   Moderate   High

6. **MINDFULNESS SKILLS:** "Be here now!"

   1   2   3   4   5   6   (7)   8   9   10
   Low   Moderate   High

7. **PROBLEM-SOLVING SKILLS:** "What is your problem?" "What are your plans?" "What is the best plan?" "Act on your plan." "How did you do?"

1	2	3	(4)	5	6	7	8	9	10
Low				Moderate					High

8. **SELF-MONITORING SKILLS:** "Think before you act"

1	2	3	4	5	6	7	8	(9)	10
Low				Moderate					High

9. **COGNITIVE FLEXIBILITY SKILLS:** "Go with the flow"

1	2	(3)	4	5	6	7	8	9	10
Low				Moderate					High

10. **OPTIMISM SKILLS:** "Hope for the future"

1	2	(3)	4	5	6	7	8	9	10
Low				Moderate					High

11. **HUMOR SKILLS:** "Laugh and the world laughs with you"

1	2	3	4	(5)	6	7	8	9	10
Low				Moderate					High

12. **RESILIENCY SKILLS:** "You can bounce back"

1	(2)	3	4	5	6	7	8	9	10
Low				Moderate					High

13. **GRATITUDE SKILLS:** "Be thankful for what you have"

1	2	3	4	5	6	7	(8)	9	10
Low				Moderate					High

14. **SUPPORTIVE SYSTEM SKILLS:** "Connect with family, friends and community"

1	2	3	4	5	6	7	(8)	9	10
Low				Moderate					High

15. **LOVING SKILLS:** "Do unto others as you would have them do unto you"

1	2	3	4	5	6	7	8	(9)	10
Low				Moderate					High

16. **SPIRITUALITY SKILLS:** Emuna "One's unconditional faith in G-d" (or higher power)

1	2	3	4	5	6	7	8	(9)	10
Low				Moderate					High

Please have your patient take some time to rate their fortitude scales with the help of a significant other in their life. Someone close to them may be able to recognize their strengths more easily than they can, especially if they have a tendency to minimize them.

- What are your patient's strengths and how do they help them reduce chronic pain?
- What are the areas that they need to strengthen to help themselves reduce their pain?
- Can your patient think of ways to strengthen these areas?

FORTITUDE SCALE

NAME: _____   DATE: _____

Please review your present experiences of the conditions noted below and rate on a scale of 1 –
10 the degree to which you believe each condition has an impact on your level of pain.

Note: The higher the rating, the stronger the belief.

**If you have a significant other person in your life, please consider asking him/her to help
you rate this scale.**
(1 = I do not believe this to be true) to (10 = I do believe this to be true)

1. **COPING SKILLS:** "You can handle it"

1	2	3	4	5	6	7	8	9	10
Low				Moderate					High

2. **SELF-ESTEEM:** "Feel good about yourself"
   Balance between

   A. SELF-CARE SKILLS "Take care of yourself"

1	2	3	4	5	6	7	8	9	10
Low				Moderate					High

   And B. SELF-EFFICACY SKILLS "Accomplish things

1	2	3	4	5	6	7	8	9	10
Low				Moderate					High

3. **ASSERTIVENESS SKILLS:** "Stand up for your rights"

1	2	3	4	5	6	7	8	9	10
Low				Moderate					High

4. **EXERCISE SKILLS:** "Just do it!"

1	2	3	4	5	6	7	8	9	10
Low				Moderate					High

5. **DISTRACTION SKILLS:** "Take the time to smell the roses"

1	2	3	4	5	6	7	8	9	10
Low				Moderate					High

6. **MINDFULNESS SKILLS:** "Be here now!"

1	2	3	4	5	6	7	8	9	10
Low				Moderate					High

7. **PROBLEM-SOLVING SKILLS:** "What is your problem?" "What are your plans?" "What is the best plan?" "Act on your plan." "How did you do?"

1	2	3	4	5	6	7	8	9	10
Low				Moderate					High

8. **SELF-MONITORING SKILLS:** "Think before you act"

1	2	3	4	5	6	7	8	9	10
Low				Moderate					High

9. **COGNITIVE FLEXIBILITY SKILLS:** "Go with the flow"

1	2	3	4	5	6	7	8	9	10
Low				Moderate					High

10. **OPTIMISM SKILLS:** "Hope for the future"

1	2	3	4	5	6	7	8	9	10
Low				Moderate					High

11. **HUMOR SKILLS:** "Laugh and the world laughs with you"

1	2	3	4	5	6	7	8	9	10
Low				Moderate					High

12. **RESILIENCY SKILLS:** "You can bounce back"

1	2	3	4	5	6	7	8	9	10
Low				Moderate					High

13. **GRATITUDE SKILLS:** "Be thankful for what you have"

1	2	3	4	5	6	7	8	9	10
Low				Moderate					High

14. **SUPPORTIVE SYSTEM SKILLS:** "Connect with family, friends and community"

1	2	3	4	5	6	7	8	9	10
Low				Moderate					High

15. **LOVING SKILLS:** "Do unto others as you would have them do unto you"

1	2	3	4	5	6	7	8	9	10
Low				Moderate					High

16. **SPIRITUALITY SKILLS:** Emuna "One's unconditional faith in G-d" (or higher power)

1	2	3	4	5	6	7	8	9	10
Low				Moderate					High

In these chapters, you have learned ten facts about your patient's chronic pain.

To review:

- Your patient's chronic pain is not new. The intensity of it is.
- Your patient's chronic pain is subjective. It is based on how your patient experiences it.
- Each patient's pain is different from another patient's pain. No two patients will experience pain the same way.
- Your patient's pain is multi-dimensional. It may consist of their physical pain, their emotional pain, their pain from life stressors, their pain from negative thinking, and their pain from a lack of fortitude.
- Your patient may always have chronic pain. What may change is the intensity of it.
- Some of your patient's coping strategies may be better than others. Your patient can now determine which strategies aren't the most helpful for them.
- Your patient must let go of "the way they were" before chronic pain. To hold on to wishing that their pain would disappear is to deny that their lives have changed dramatically since having chronic pain.
- Each patient may differ from all your other patients in their motivation to change the ways in which they are coping.
- Times are changing rapidly, and this impacts how your patient deals with their pain.
- Your patients are free to choose the ways they use to lower their chronic pain. There are many strategies available for them to try out.

My intention in presenting these facts to you is to help your patients see their chronic pain as a "challenge" and as an "opportunity" to grow and overcome it, rather than a reason to despair. Since your patient's pain is multi-dimensional, it is unrealistic for you, as a healthcare provider, to simply say to them, "On a scale of 1 to 10, what is your pain level?" They will share with you their subjective level of physical pain. But, they may also have pain from their emotional states, pain from life stressors, pain from negative thinking, or pain from a lack of fortitude. To change their perspective of chronic pain in a positive way, I have showed you how your patients can use five different scales that measure the multiple dimensions of their chronic pain over time. You've seen examples of how different patients experienced their chronic pain and then measured it on each scale. In the next chapter, we'll explore a "case study" of a patient who experiences chronic pain and has measured her pain levels on these five dimensions.

Doc! My whole family has been misunderstood!

Chapter 6: A Case Study

This chapter presents you with an opportunity to read a short "case study" of a patient named Joanna who experiences chronic pain and has measured her pain levels on all given dimensions. After reading about Joanna's situation, you will see how she rated herself on all five scales, and I'll ask you to see if you can come up with ways to help her. Then you can compare your strategies with specific strategies I share with you in the subsequent chapters to help your patients, like Joanna, reduce their chronic pain.

Joanna is a 48-year-old married woman with two children who experiences heightened anxiety and severe chronic, physical pain on her left ankle following a recent fall on a piece of ice in her driveway. She is overweight and physically inactive much of the time, and was so even before the fall, except for driving her children to and from local activities. Two years ago, she had surgery on a tendon stretching from her right elbow to her right shoulder. She has finally obtained disability insurance for her constant pain and anxiety (which included ongoing panic attacks). Prior to obtaining disability, she had lost her full-time job as a veterinarian technician because of frequent absences due to both anxiety and pain.

After the recent fall, Joanna's husband, Mike, took her immediately to the hospital emergency room where an X-ray revealed that she had several ankle bone fragmentations. The ER staff recommended that she immediately see her medical team. In turn, her clinical nurse practitioner referred Joanna to an orthopedic surgeon who surgically inserted a plate with screws to stabilize her ankle. Joanna returned home two days later with crutches and a seven-day prescription for Vicodin. After four weeks of home care (including nursing, physical and occupational therapy) she met again with her orthopedic surgeon. Another X-ray revealed that one of the stabilizing plate screws had loosened, but the surgeon didn't believe that would cause her any additional pain. He informed Joanna and Mike that he wouldn't remove the plate until the bones could solidify and she could increase her mobility through ongoing physical therapy. The surgeon further recommended that Joanna wean herself off the Vicodin and stick to taking NSAIDS like ibuprofen or naproxen or use acetaminophen.

For the next three months, Joanna did little to improve her condition. She continued to feel much pain but secretly obtained opiates from an acquaintance. After home services stopped, Joanna scheduled physical therapy appointments but often cancelled them at the last minute because she was in "too much pain." She did little to exercise or stretch and became more depressed while continuing to secretly take opiates, and she spent much of her time lying in bed. At one point, her husband thought about taking her back to the ER because she had expressed some suicidal thoughts. When he discovered that Joanna was using street opiates, he made an emergency appointment with her primary care physician, who recommended a detoxification program. Joanna's physician further recommended that, once she was detoxed, she consider getting on methadone or Suboxone (buprenorphine), attend a weekly clinic, then meet with the team's clinician to address where she was in her motivation to change.

Joanna did these things and saw the clinician the following week. He listened attentively and without judgment to Joanna's concerns and how she presently dealt with her pain. He expressed empathy for how she had been enduring pain, even before her fall.

The clinician obtained Joanna's permission to collaborate with Mike to make sure Joanna weaned herself off the opiates over time. She also attended an outpatient drug treatment program for at least two weeks in addition to her medication clinic. She further agreed to see her clinician in the late afternoons.

The clinician then questioned Joanna, without judgment and without giving advice, about the ways she was choosing to cope with her pain. He wondered how her choices had been both helpful and harmful for reducing pain.

Together, they did a cost-benefit analysis of her present methods, including the use of opiates, being overweight, keeping physical therapy appointments inconsistently, and being anxious and idle. The clinician emphasized the need for Joanna to consider both the short-term and long-term consequences of her choices. By doing this, Joanna realized that most of her present strategies for reducing pain were not effective, especially her reliance on opiates. She acknowledged that she had to let go of these choices but the real issue for her was that she let go of thinking about how happy she had been before the onset of her chronic pain.

During the next few sessions, the clinician helped Joanna mourn how she was in the past prior to having severe pain. Together, they worked through each grief stage until Joanna could come to terms with accepting that she might always have pain, but it didn't have to be so intolerable.

Next, the clinician explained to Joanna how chronic pain is multi-dimensional, that it is subjective (meaning each person's experience of pain is different), and that pain is a metaphor for all kinds of pain, including one's emotional states, life stressors, negative thinking, and the degree to which one uses one's strengths to deal with chronic pain. He told Joanna that she could reframe her chronic pain as a challenge and as an opportunity to test her strengths in dealing with life changes.

He brought out the Chronic Pain Scales, reviewed the instructions for each one, including how to score them, then explained that the overall goal was to do whatever it took to reduce the negative pain scale ratings to between 1 and 4 and increase the positive scale ratings to between 7 and 10, weekly over time. He offered her the same strategies to reduce chronic pain that are provided in the next few chapters, and explained that "one size doesn't fit all." What would work for her would be different than what worked for other people who had chronic pain. The strategies that people choose needed to be acted upon on a trial basis. If one or some didn't work, then Joanna should try others.

The clinician told Joanna that it would be helpful if she could review the strategies at home with Mike, then choose the ones she planned to use. He asked if she could complete the five scales at least twice during the week, then meet again the following week to see if they noticed any patterns. Joanna agreed to complete the scales at home with her husband's assistance and to bring them back to the clinician at periodic check-ins every few weeks after the next week's appointment.

PHYSICAL PAIN SCALE (1 DAY)

NAME: Joanna

DATE: 6|8|17

Please rate your physical pain during a day, per hour, on a scale from 1-10. Please describe what you are doing, the location of the pain, whether it is constant or comes and goes, and what the pain is like using the adjectives on the next page.

TIME: 12:00 PM   1   2   3   4   (5)   6   7   8   9   10

                Low Pain   Moderate Pain   Intense Pain

Left ankle, Just get home, walked upstairs and around house
Pain is constant, it's a sharp aching pain, took 800mg ibupr

TIME: 2:12 pm   1   2   3   (4)   5   6   7   8   9   10

                Low Pain   Moderate Pain   Intense Pain

Left ankle just did dishes and made a tuna sandwich for
myself, Pain is constant and its still flickering with each step

TIME: 3:20 pm   1   2   3   4   (5)   6   7   8   9   10
left ankle + achilles   Low Pain   Moderate Pain   Intense Pain
          tendon

Just did got back from dropping daughter off Walk and
climbing stairs, Pain is sharp aching

TIME: 4:30 pm   1   2   3   (4)   5   6   7   8   9   10

                Low Pain   Moderate Pain   Intense Pain

Left ankle, right elbow. Been lying down watching TV. Pain ease
a little, To a dull ache, right elbow starting to ache (Had tennis elbow
surgery 2 yrs ago still bothers me)

TIME: 5:20 pm   1   2   3   4   (5)   6   7   8   9   10

                Low Pain   Moderate Pain   Intense Pain

Want to get AC in my car charged, ankle really sore.
Now a sharp aching all around my ankle.

TIME: 6:40 pm   1   2   3   4   5   (6)   7   8   9   10
                   Low Pain   Moderate Pain   Intense Pain

Left ankle. Ate half of a dry steak bomb. for supper, settling down for the night. Tingling and aching pain. Took 800 mg of Ibuprofen

TIME: 7:45 pm   1   2   3   4   5   (6)   7   8   9   10
                   Low Pain   Moderate Pain   Intense Pain

Left ankle and leg Watching 3rd season of Prison Break, overall left ankle very sore, radiating up my legs, NT as helped as it was earlier

TIME: 8:55 pm   1   2   3   4   5   (6)   7   8   9   10
                   Low Pain   Moderate Pain   Intense Pain

Left ankle watching TV, have leg up on 3 pillows, pain is aching around ankle

Some words that can help you describe the way your pain feels. Is it ___

Aching?	Cramping?	Taut?	Crippling?	Gnawing?
Freezing?	Unbearable?	Heavy?	Hot or burning?	Nagging?
Numb?	Sharp? ✓	Shooting?	Squeezing?	Cold?
Sickening?	Splitting?	Tight?	Dreadful?	Stabbing? ✓
Punishing or cruel?	Cool?	Bolts?	Tender?	Throbbing?
Agonizing?	Excruciating?	Tiring?	Distressing?	Stiffness?
Pulling?	Flickering?	Pricking?	Pinching?	Vicious?
Mild?	Intense?	Pulsing?	Intermittent?	Scalding?
Exhausting?	Sore?	Wretched?	Terrifying?	Killing?
Beating?	Jumping?	Miserable?	Piercing?	Drilling?
Cutting?	Tearing?	Nauseating?	Constant?	Stinging?
Electrical?	Pounding?	Tugging?	Penetrating?	Knot-like?
Horrible?	Smarting?	Pins/Needles?	Radiating? ✓	Varying?
Rasping?	Annoying?	Quivering?	Itchy?	Suffocating?
Spreading?	Dull? ✓	Tingling? ✓	Grueling?	Drawing?

PHYSICAL PAIN SCALE (2 DAY)

Please rate your physical pain for **2 days during the morning, afternoon and evening** on a scale from 1-10. Please describe what you are doing, the location of the pain, whether it is constant, or comes and goes, and what the pain is like using the adjectives on the next page.

DATE: 6|10|17

Morning   Time: 8am

1 (2) 3   4   5   6   7   8   9   10
Low Pain   Moderate Pain   Intense Pain

Just get up less when relaxed from evening - mild in left ankle

Afternoon   Time: 1PM

1   2   3   4   5   6 (7) 8   9   10
Low Pain   Moderate Pain   Intense Pain

Walking w. that friend, had to stop a lot of pain in left ankle; piercing, sharp

Evening   Time: 8pm

1   2   3   4   5   6 (7) 8   9   10
Low Pain   Moderate Pain   Intense Pain

Still in pain from doing dishes, fatigue, right elbow w/ stinging dull ache, left ankle, sharp

DATE: 6|12|17

Morning   Time: 7:30 Am

1   2 (3) 4   5   6   7   8   9   10
Low Pain   Moderate Pain   Intense Pain

Less pain, sleep helps as does not moving Dull, numb

Afternoon   Time: _11:30 AM_

    1   2   3   4   5   6   7 (8) 9   10
    Low Pain   Moderate Pain   Intense Pain

Really hurts, tried to walk for a mile, left ankle, sharp, stinging elbow or when don't lift anything

Evening   Time: _8:00 PM_

    1   2   3   4   5   6 (7) 8   9   10
    Low Pain   Moderate Pain   Intense Pain

Leg and ankle pain is intense constant, try to do some housework, right elbow, also stabbing from using utensils.

Some words that can help you describe the way your pain feels. Is it ___

Aching? ✓	Cramping?	Taut?	Crippling?	Gnawing? ✓
Freezing?	Unbearable?	Heavy?	Hot or burning?	Nagging?
Numb? ✓	Sharp? ✓	Shooting? ✓	Squeezing?	Cold?
Sickening?	Splitting?	Tight?	Dreadful?	Stabbing? ✓
Punishing or cruel?	Cool?	Bolts?	Tender? ✓	Throbbing? ✓
Agonizing? ✓	Excruciating?	Tiring?	Distressing?	Stiffness?
Pulling?	Flickering?	Pricking?	Pinching?	Vicious?
Mild? ✓	Intense? ✓	Pulsing?	Intermittent?	Scalding?
Exhausting?	Sore? ✓	Wretched?	Terrifying?	Killing?
Beating?	Jumping?	Miserable?	Piercing?	Drilling?
Cutting?	Tearing?	Nauseating?	Constant? ✓	Stinging?
Electrical?	Pounding?	Tugging? ✓	Penetrating?	Knot-like?
Horrible?	Smarting?	Pins/Needles?	Radiating?	Varying?
Rasping?	Annoying?	Quivering?	Itchy?	Suffocating?
Spreading?	Dull?	Tingling? ✓	Grueling?	Drawing?

LIFE STRESS PAIN SCALE

Please review your present experiences of stress below and rate on a scale of 1-10 the degree to which you believe each stressor impacts your pain. (1 is no impact, 10 is strong impact.)

If you have a significant other person in your life, please consider asking him/her to help you complete the ratings for this scale.

NAME: Joanna   DATE: 6|8|17

- ❏ Housing
- ❏ Engagement
- ❏ Pregnancy
- ☑ Teenagers 8
- ❏ In-laws
- ❏ Hobbies
- ❏ Single
- ❏ Hours at Work
- ☑ Finances 9
- ❏ Rape
- ❏ Natural Catastrophe
- ❏ Caring for Elder(s)
- ❏ Legal Issues
- ☑ Insurance Concerns 9
- ❏ Workman's Compensation
- ❏ Experiencing/ Witnessing/Hearing About Trama
- ❏ Education

- ☑ Relationships 7
- ❏ Childbirth
- ❏ Parents
- ❏ Friendships
- ❏ Affair(s)
- ❏ Post-Marital Conflict
- ❏ Increased Work Responsibilities
- ❏ Wills/Estates
- ❏ Death of Loved One
- ❏ Lack of Assertiveness
- ☑ Substance Use/ 10 Abuse/Dependence
- ☑ Medical Issues 8
- ❏ Getting/ Not Getting Disability Insurance
- ❏ Retirement
- ❏ Isolation

- ❏ Marital Problems
- ❏ Children's Illness
- ❏ Role Functions
- ❏ Social Life
- ❏ Separation
- ❏ Single Parenting
- ❏ Multi-Tasking Demands
- ☑ Aging 7
- ❏ Grandparenting
- ❏ Religious Affiliation
- ❏ Other Addictions (Phone, Internet, Gambling, Porn)
- ❏ Hospitalization(s)
- ❏ Listening to or Watching News
- ❏ Dating
- ❏ Infertility
- ❏ Raising Children

- ❏ Siblings
- ❏ Lack of Exercise
- ❏ Divorce
- ❏ Balancing Parenting and work
- ❏ Career Issues/ Dissatisfaction
- ❏ War
- ❏ Unemployment
- ❏ Verbal or Physical Abuse
- ❏ Getting into an Accident (with/without) injuries
- ☑ Surgery(ies) 9
- ❏ Politics
- ❏ Other:
- _____
- _____
- _____

Please indicate the average rating of your present stressors between 7 and 10 that impact your pain. Add up only items rated from 7 to 10 and divide the total by the number of items counted to find your average rating.

1	2	3	4	5	6	7	⑧	9	10
Not a problem				Somewhat of a problem				A very large problem	

Next, rate the impact of that level of life stress on your

Family (1-10)	Work (1-10)	Social Life (1-10)
9	10	8

104

EMOTIONAL PAIN SCALE

NAME: Joanna   DATE: 6|8|17

Please review your present experiences of the emotional conditions noted below and rate on a scale of 1 – 10 the degree to which you believe each one has an impact on your level of pain.

If you have a significant other person in your life please consider asking him/her to help you rate this scale.
(1 = I do not believe this to be true) to (10 = I do believe this to be true)

*(**Note:** Happiness Scale is scored differently than the other three scales - the higher the score, the better the rating)*

1. **DEPRESSION:**

1	2	3	4	5	6	(7)	8	9	10
	Low			Moderate			Severe		
	(low-sad-hurt)			(unhappy-aggrieved-dejected)			(depressed-miserable-despondent)		

2. **ANXIETY:**

1	2	3	4	5	6	7	(8)	9	10
	Low			Moderate			Severe		
(concerned-uncomfortable-bothered)			(worried-upset-troubled)			(frightened-overwhelmed-panicky)		

3. **ANGER:**

1	(2)	3	4	5	6	7	8	9	10
	Low			Moderate			Severe		
(annoyed-hurt-disappointed)			(frustrated-upset-mad)			(furious-enraged-incensed)		

4. **HAPPINESS:**

1	(2)	3	4	5	6	7	8	9	10
	Low			Moderate			Severe		
(glad-comfortable-content)			(cheerful-pleased-happy)			(blissful-exhilarated-ecstatic)		

COGNITIVE APPRAISAL OF PAIN SCALE

NAME: Joanna   DATE: 6|8|17

Please rate these different cognitive appraisals on a scale of 1-10 to the degree to which you believe each appraisal to be true for you.

If you have a significant other person in your life please consider asking him/her to help you rate this scale.

(1 = I do not believe this to be true) to (10 = I do believe this to be true)

1. **ALL OR NOTHING (DICHOTOMOUS) THINKING:**
    You view most situations as falling into one of two distinct categories (always vs. never, perfect vs. terrible). How often do you catch yourself making statements like, "I can't work because I always have pain" or, "I never feel good"?

1	2	3	4	5	6	7	8	(9)	10
A little				Some					A Lot

2. **OVER GENERALIZATION:**
    You reach more global negative conclusions that go well beyond the one situation. How often do these kinds of thoughts sound familiar to you? "I can't do what I used to do because I can't bike" or, "I won't be able to do anything because I can't walk long distances."

1	2	3	4	5	6	7	8	9	(10)
A little				Some					A Lot

3. **MENTAL FILTERING:**
    You pay more attention to a single detail instead of seeing the whole picture. How often do you think something like, "My pain means that I'm inadequate" or, "I couldn't go shopping today means that I'm not good enough"?

1	2	3	4	5	6	7	8	(9)	10
A little				Some					A Lot

4. **DISQUALIFYING THE POSITIVE:**
    You tell yourself that positive experiences don't count. How often do you think something like, "I was able to cook one meal last night but one night out of twenty doesn't mean much"?

1	2	3	4	5	6	7	8	9	(10)
A little				Some					A Lot

5. **JUMPING TO CONCLUSIONS - FUTURISTIC THINKING:**
    You focus on the future and predict it negatively without considering other possibilities. How often do you think this kind of thought? "Oh no! Here comes the pain again. I'll definitely wind up in the emergency ward."

1	2	3	4	5	6	(7)	8	9	10
A little				Some					A Lot

6. **CATASTROPHIZING - MAGNIFICATION:**
    You exaggerate the importance of negative things and minimize the positive, focusing on the worst-case scenario versus the best-case scenario. You make a mountain out of a molehill. How often do you think of these kinds of thoughts? "My pain will be totally unbearable" or, "I can't handle this anymore!"

1	2	3	4	5	6	7	(8)	9	10
A little				Some					A Lot

Adapted by the author from materials by Aaron Beck, MD

7. EMOTIONAL REASONING:

You think that if you feel something so strongly, then it must be true. How often do you think these kinds of negative thoughts? "I don't care what my physical therapist says! I feel that it can't be good for me" or, "I feel that it's going to be painful."

1	2	3	4	5	6	(7)	8	9	10
A little				Some					A Lot

8. "SHOULD" STATEMENTS:

You hold fixed ideas as to how the world ought to, or must be true. (This may relate to high self-standards.) How often do you have thoughts like, "I should be able to walk 5 miles" or, "Everyone should understand why I can't exercise" or, "I have to take strong pain medications"?

1	2	3	4	5	6	7	8	(9)	10
A little				Some					A Lot

9. LABELING:

You attach a global, extreme negative label to yourself or others. How often do you catch yourself making judgments like these? "I'm stupid!" or, "I'm not good enough!" or, "All doctors are uncaring jerks!"

1	2	3	4	5	6	7	(8)	9	(10)
A little				Some					A Lot

10. NEED FOR CONTROL:

You believe that you must control everything in your life; yourself, your relationships, your emotions, or your personal situations. How often do you have thoughts like these? "I need to know everything about what's going to happen" or, "The need to control helps me to not feel helpless and powerless."

1	2	3	4	5	6	7	8	(9)	10
A little				Some					A Lot

11. PERSONALIZATION:

You believe you're responsible for negative situations and that it is all your fault, even when there is no evidence to indicate that this is true. How often do you catch yourself thinking statements like these? "This pain is punishment for something I did wrong" or, "If I don't have pain, then my spouse wouldn't be mad at me."

1	2	(3)	4	5	6	7	8	9	10
A little				Some					A Lot

12. UNDERESTIMATING YOUR STRENGTHS:

You minimize the positive traits that you have to handle your pain. How often do you have these kinds of thoughts? "I can't handle my pain" or, "It's not worth trying anymore."

1	2	3	4	5	6	7	8	(9)	10
A little				Some					A Lot

13. MIND READING:

You think that the other person is having specific thoughts about you and your pain. How often do you have these kinds of thoughts? "My spouse thinks that I can't do anything because of my pain" or, "My friend thinks that I'm not doing enough to help myself."

1	2	3	4	5	6	7	(8)	9	10
A little				Some					A Lot

Adapted by the author from materials by Aaron Beck, MD

FORTITUDE SCALE

NAME: Joanna   DATE: 6/8/17

Please review your present experiences of the conditions noted below and rate on a scale of 1 – 10 the degree to which you believe each condition has an impact on your level of pain.

Note: The higher the rating, the stronger the belief.

If you have a significant other person in your life, please consider asking him/her to help you rate this scale.
(1 = I do not believe this to be true) to (10 = I do believe this to be true)

1. **COPING SKILLS:** "You can handle it"

1	2	(3)	4 .	5	6	7	8	9	10
Low				Moderate					High

2. **SELF-ESTEEM:** "Feel good about yourself"
   Balance between

   A. SELF-CARE SKILLS "Take care of yourself"

1	(2)	3	4	5	6	7	8	9	10
Low				Moderate					High

   And B. SELF-EFFICACY SKILLS "Accomplish things

1	(2)	3	4	5	6	7	8	9	10
Low				Moderate					High

3. **ASSERTIVENESS SKILLS:** "Stand up for your rights"

1	2	3	(4)	5	6	7	8	9	10
Low				Moderate					High

4. **EXERCISE SKILLS:** "Just do it!"

1	(2)	3	4	5	6	7	8	9	10
Low				Moderate					High

5. **DISTRACTION SKILLS:** "Take the time to smell the roses"

1	(2)	3	4	5	6	7	8	9	10
Low				Moderate					High

6. **MINDFULNESS SKILLS:** "Be here now!"

1	2	(3)	4	5	6	7	8	9	10
Low				Moderate					High

7. **PROBLEM SOLVING SKILLS:** "What is your problem?" "What are your plans?"
    "What is the best plan?" "Act on your plan." "How did you do?"

1	2	3	4	(5)	6	7	8	9	10
Low				Moderate					High

8. **SELF-MONITORING SKILLS:** "Think before you act"

1	2	3	(4)	5	6	7	8	9	10
Low				Moderate					High

9. **COGNITIVE FLEXIBILITY SKILLS:** "Go with the flow"

1	2	3	(4)	5	6	7	8	9	10
Low				Moderate					High

10. **OPTIMISM SKILLS:** "Hope for the future"

1	(2)	3	4	5	6	7	8	9	10
Low				Moderate					High

11. **HUMOR SKILLS:** "Laugh and the world laughs with you"

1	2	3	4	5	(6)	7	8	9	10
Low				Moderate					High

12. **RESILIENCY SKILLS:** "You can bounce back"

1	2	3	(4)	5	6	7	8	9	10
Low				Moderate					High

13. **GRATITUDE SKILLS:** "Be thankful for what you have"

1	2	3	4	(5)	6	7	8	9	10
Low				Moderate					High

14. **SUPPORTIVE SYSTEM SKILLS:** "Connect with family, friends and community"

1	2	3	4	5	6	7	8	9	10
Low				Moderate					High

15. **LOVING SKILLS:** "Do unto others as you would have them do unto you"

1	2	(X3)	4	(5)	6	7	8	9	10
Low				Moderate					High

16. **SPIRITUALITY SKILLS:** Emuna "One's unconditional faith in G-d" (or higher power)

1	2	(3)	4	5	6	7	8	9	10
Low				Moderate					High

Upon meeting with Joanna again in a week's time, the clinician first acknowledged how well she had been able to get around and do multiple daily tasks and that most of her pain rating levels between 4 and 6 weren't so bad. He further noticed that she had sharp, dull or aching pain and that it was more constant than variable. Sometimes, the pain radiated through her leg. Together, they thought that it might be helpful to first re-review this concern with her primary care physician or clinical nurse practitioner to see if she needed a referral to another specialist, such as a neurologist, a medical pain specialist like an anesthesiologist for possible injections, or perhaps a physical therapist or chiropractor. At least for now, the clinician recommended taking short breaks to ease the pain rather than wait to lie down at night when she rated the pain levels as a 3.

Joanna experienced severe depression and anxiety but had limited anger and irritability. She internalized her symptoms, which probably aggravated her pain condition. Clearly, Joanna wasn't a very happy person at this time, given her low rating of 3 on the Happiness segment of the Emotional Pain Scale.

The clinician pointed out how Joanna had multiple negative thoughts that contributed immensely to her chronic pain. She rated all the appraisals on the Cognitive Appraisal of Pain Scale high except for "Personalization," meaning she didn't necessarily blame herself excessively for her pain, although she rated "Labeling" as high. This implied that the extent of her high negative ratings on this scale contributed to Joanna having an overall negative schema or belief about herself as being "stupid" or "not good enough."

Joanna had multiple life stressors contributing to her pain. Her high ratings of how life stress was impacting work, family and relationships indicated her stressors were strong influences on how she experienced chronic pain.

Of most concern were Joanna's low scale ratings for the many areas of strength needed to reduce chronic pain. The only high rating on her Fortitude Scale was in her capacity to experience the humorous aspects of situations. While humor is a positive strength, several other areas could be more easily strengthened than others, like trying to be grateful and loving. Still, Joanna needed much help in developing critical skills like self-esteem, the capacity to cope, being resilient, optimistic and appreciative of the positive aspects of life.

If you were Joanna's clinician or healthcare professional, what specific goals would you want to identify to help lower her negative rating scales to a 1-4 and increase the positive ones to 7-10 over time? Try to think of five goals for each of the five scales, and try to help her make them as realistic as possible. You may want her to divide her goals into sub-goals, if necessary.

Physical Goals

1._____
2._____
3._____
4._____
5._____

Emotional Goals

1._____
2._____
3._____
4._____
5._____

Life Stressor Goals

1._____
2._____
3._____
4._____
5._____

Negative Thinking Goals

1. _____
2. _____
3. _____
4. _____
5. _____

Fortitude Goals

1. _____
2. _____
3. _____
4. _____
5. _____

Ponder your next move carefully.

Chapter 7: Overall Strategies to Reduce Your Patients' Chronic Pain

Now that you've read Joanna's story (in the previous chapter) and have written down suggested goals for her, I want you to read the specific strategies I identify in the next few chapters, and determine which strategies would be helpful for Joanna, and for your patients.

There are many ways to explore how to reduce your patients' physical pain. Your patients may find that the strategies below are a great place to start. Your patients will benefit from what I have learned to try first to reduce their chronic pain. Review these ideas, and then read about specific strategies your patients may want to try for each pain scale.

There are two major stages to pain reduction. The first is pain loss or doing whatever it takes to reduce pain. The second is pain maintenance or preventing relapses of pain flare-ups over time. This would be defined as ratings of 1-4 for negative scaled items on the Physical Pain Scale, the Life Stress Pain Scale, the Emotional Pain Scale, and the Cognitive Appraisal of Pain Scale, and ratings of 7-10 for positive scaled items on the Emotional and Fortitude Scales. Your patients need to know their specific triggers that can increase their pain flare-ups, especially those triggers that can increase negative thoughts. Of course, there are situations your patients can't control, such as some major life stressors.

In all areas of behavior change -- whether it be reducing your patients' pain, their weight, their diabetes, their cholesterol levels, or their abuse of alcohol, opiates, tobacco or cannabis (beyond what has been prescribed for medical purposes) -- the most critical elements of success are your patients having sufficient support systems in place and the ability to keep knowing which of their triggers can induce relapses. In fact, relapse prevention is just as important as pain reduction. The goal is to reduce and maintain your patients' negative pain scale ratings, improve their positive ones, and then sustain them, keeping their rating levels steady over time.

Your patients' inability to maintain their behavior change over time is why most of their plans often fail. For example, many of your patients may go on a diet, then regain their lost weight. Why? Because they don't have maintenance strategies in place to keep their weight within a reasonable range over time. The same is often true when it comes to chronic pain reduction and painless maintenance. Your patients must have strategies and support in place for them to succeed!

Remember, there is a difference between your patients controlling their pain and having no pain. They may always have pain, when they consider that their physical pain is impacted by multiple factors, like their emotions, life stressors, negative thoughts and fortitude, or lack thereof.

While it is critical to help your patients establish and maintain support systems, no one else can truly appreciate the level of pain they experience, not even their closest loved ones. Still, your patients must do everything they can to involve them in their Pain Management Lifestyle. Your patients must educate others about what their pain is like, when they have it, and what they are doing to reduce it. It may be helpful for your patients to have people in their support systems attend a session with you or another member of their pain management team, so they can learn what your patients are going through and how they are trying to overcome these experiences by committing to certain strategies. Have support system members understand that your patients are grieving the loss of how they once were before they had high pain intensity. Your patients may want to ask their support system members to be understanding if they "lose it" once in a while, as it is common for them to experience high levels of anxiety, anger or depression.

Helpful Strategies for Your Patients
to Maintain Their Pain Reduction Over Time

Here's a list of seven strategies for your patients to use in their own Pain Management Lifestyle as they focus on reducing their pain to the degree that they can and learn other ways to manage the pain that remains.

1. Have your patients use the five pain scales provided in this book to help them self-monitor how they are doing on a weekly basis. Have them note what needs to be reduced (to a level between 1 and 4) and what needs to improve (to a level between 7 and 10), then have them plan and act on ways to do so over time. Remember that their pain scale results are snapshots of what their experience is at that moment in time. Have them make copies of the scales in Chapters 8 through 12 (or email the author at drgeorgepainless@gmail.com to obtain copies) and have them complete the scales at least once weekly to see how they are doing.

2. Advise your patients to know what their high-scoring negative thoughts tend to be, especially those that trigger emotional pain (anxiety, depression and anger). In Chapter 11, you will learn how to help your patients generate rational thoughts to combat these emotions.

3. Have your patients use their heads! That is, have them improve the use of their prefrontal cortex, especially their specific executive functions of self-monitoring (catching themselves generating negative thoughts), cognitive flexibility (shifting and adjusting when upsets occur), healthy problem-solving, and practicing specific fortitude skills.

4. Encourage your patients to have support systems in place. Have them review their progress regularly with you and members of their pain management team. The clinician working with them on the Pain Management Lifestyle Model should primarily be a health psychologist, a social worker or a licensed mental health counselor with particular experience and training in pain management. This is especially true if you or other healthcare providers on the team (or if you are an auxiliary provider) don't have the time. Encourage your patients to join support groups, take

advantage of helpful websites and social media groups, and learn from other people who are also trying to reduce their chronic pain.

5. Make sure that your patients' caretaker(s), whether they be spouses, cohabiters or best friends, obtain enough support through good self-care practices. Your patients don't want to burn out these important people! The significant others in patients' lives need support as well, and they need to take care of themselves. Your patients don't want to criticize, alienate or lose them. Rather, your patients should respect that their caretakers need refueling through their own support systems and need to take the time to engage in their preferred self-care activities. Your patients should keep their caretakers regularly apprised of how they are doing. They should meet regularly with you and the rest of their pain management team to stay informed and provide you with input that helps them collaborate effectively with you to tailor pain reduction and maintenance strategies to their needs.

6. Advise your patients to go slowly! Have them set realistic expectations and measure them through sub-goals, rather than expect a dramatic change from one level of their pain scales to another. If they become frustrated, it is probably due to their having high self-standards or not fully letting go of what they used to be capable of doing before chronic pain entered their lives.

7. Have your patients maintain the strategies that they, you and other members of their pain management team have chosen. Continue to monitor how they are helping or not helping your patients to reduce their negative pain scale ratings and improve their positive ones. Encourage your patients to change or modify these strategies if they're not finding them to be effective. One size doesn't fit all!

Now that we've taken a broad overview of pain management strategies, let's turn next to specific ways your patients can reduce their pain in each of the five areas (physical, life stressors, emotional, negative thoughts, and fortitude) measured by the scales.

You are your own SUPER person.

Chapter 8: Physical Ways to Reduce Your Patients' Chronic Pain

"Of pain you could wish only one thing: that it should stop.
Nothing in the world was so bad as physical pain.
In the face of pain there are no heroes."
- George Orwell

The recommendations I include in this chapter are the ones I found the most helpful, both as a professional who has worked with patients who experience chronic pain and as someone who personally has had chronic pain. It is important to realize that the majority of your professional peers will focus on physical recommendations, like the ones in this chapter, rather than on the recommendations suggested in the next few chapters that focus on other critical ways to help reduce your patient's pain.

1. Don't encourage your patients to stay in bed! It's very easy for them to hunker down, pull the covers over their bodies and rest their heads on a soft pillow to withdraw from the reality of having to get up and face another day of chronic pain. Just as tempting is

the notion of sitting in a chair all day watching TV and eating to their hearts' content while becoming more depressed or anxious. Yes, these activities may feel good and comfy, and it's their choice! But it's not the best choice, either in the short or the long term. They'll experience greater stiffness, muscle atrophy and pain from discs that fill up with fluid while lying down and hurt when they get up. Staying in bed will cause the significant others in your patients' lives to become concerned or even frustrated and angry. Avoidance and withdrawal are coping techniques but they're not the best ways to reduce chronic pain.

2. Encourage your patients to get better sleep. Do they sleep poorly? Have a hard time getting to sleep? Do they get up frequently? Do they still feel tired in the morning? Is it difficult for them to get between seven and nine hours of sleep and feel rested in the morning? These problems can be caused by simple things like eating or using electronic devices too close to bedtime, or drinking too much caffeine or alcohol. Poor sleep can correlate highly with stress, anxiety, and depression, or a combination of these factors.

    If obtaining good sleep is your patients' problem, then they should tell you and other pain management team members so you can help them determine what's going on. Reviewing their different pain scale ratings will help them identify what may be affecting their sleep. In some instances, your patients' sleep problems may be caused by other medical problems or a combination of factors. For example, being overweight may be related to having sleep apnea. If it's possible for them, then you may request a sleep study. If you discover that they have even moderate sleep apnea, then they should get the newest versions of the CPAP machine. As awkward as it may feel, your patients will notice incredible differences not only in their ability to fall asleep but also in their ability to stay asleep without getting up all the time (even to urinate). Their snoring will diminish, and they will feel incredibly rested in the morning. They will even be able to sleep in the same bed again with their spouse or significant other!

3. Does your patient have a comfortable bed? Is it too hard? Too soft? Too small? Personally, I found that a hard mattress gave me incredible muscle spasms in the morning. Make sure your patients' beds feel comfortable to them and provide far less pain while they sleep and when they awaken.

4. Suggest that your patients develop a morning ritual, using these ideas as a template. When they get up in the morning, suggest they do the following:

- Meditate, do a mindfulness exercise, or pray for at least 10 minutes.
- Identify five things or people for which or to whom they are forever grateful. This will help them keep a sense of perspective. Some days their list may simply include the fact that they are still alive and breathing or that their situation could be worse!
- Listen to some relaxing or inspiring music as they get out of bed. It will soothe their souls.
- Massage out any stiffness in their muscles by using a foam roller. It's like having your own masseuse.
- Stretch, doing only those warm-up stretches before and/or after they do any aerobic exercises (fast walking, swimming, biking) that you or their pain management team healthcare providers have recommended. Certain stretches can do more harm than good, depending on a person's physical ailments. Your patients might try elastic exercise bands for a variety of stretches. It's a wonderful tool for improving their flexibility and strength.

5. There will be times when you need to refer your patients to specialists. A referral may be necessary to clarify the causes of any clear physical conditions that could be exacerbating their pain. You and your pain management team members should be the primary authorities to determine what medical tests need to be done and what specialists a patient should be authorized to see.

6. Have your patients seek multiple solutions. There is no single solution and no easy way to reduce chronic pain. Physical pain can come simply from poor posture and movement patterns. Core strengthening, building mobility and endurance, and keeping to extension or inflexion movements that reduce pain, not aggravate

it, is critical. Again, it is best for patients to have a full-range workup to determine which postures or movements cause them the most pain, then help them identify specific exercises that will be most helpful.

7. Help your patients know what's enough! There is a distinction between their "doing too much" and "doing too little" to obtain medical evidence that supports a clear physical cause for their pain that may need specific treatments, or surgery in some cases. What is "enough" should be based on a realistic appraisal by you and other pain management team members. It should not be based on your patients getting caught up in all-or-nothing thinking (known as a negative cognitive appraisal) or trying to meet unrealistic standards. It's always more of a relief for them to find a clear physical cause for their chronic pain, but remember that their pain is subjective, multidimensional, and influenced by other factors that can increase pain. These other factors include their coexisting depression, anxiety, anger, lack of happiness, life stressors, negative thoughts, and lack of fortitude. If they don't consider these additional factors on an ongoing basis, then they'll be constantly searching for a physical cause.

8. Have your patients maintain multiple strategies that you and the pain management team have chosen. Be sure your patients continue to monitor how these strategies are helping or not helping them reduce their negative pain scale ratings and improve their positive ones. Help your patients change strategies if the current ones are not helping. One size doesn't fit all.

9. Your patients should not rely on opiates as a major way to reduce their chronic pain. While some of your patients may need to be on opiates for some time, all of your patients should be aware that you and other pain management team professionals are reducing or eliminating opiate prescriptions due to the exponential increase in deaths from opiate overdoses. Even if you are an anesthesiologist trained in pain management, and you do trigger point injections, nerve blocks, neural ablations (nerve burning) and insert transcutaneous electronic nerve stimulators (internal TENS devices), you are now veering away from prescribing opiates. There are other medications that can help

with your patients' pain. These include NSAIDS (like aspirin, ibuprofen and naproxen), acetaminophen, selective serotonin norepinephrine reuptake inhibitors (SSNRIs), and other tricyclic antidepressants (TCAs). For a longer-term basis, you may consider buprenorphine (Suboxone) or methadone. Still, it is always best for you to consider recommending multiple pain reduction strategies that may possibly include medications, rather than having your patients depend solely on them.

10. Make sure your patients build their own support team. When they are in the preparation stage of change, they should consider the importance of building their support networks. They should strongly consider the benefits of remaining engaged, as long as they can, in physical ways to increase their strength and mobility. This usually means they have consistent meetings with a specialist who is well trained and experienced in the physical conditions of their bodies. If you recommend a trainer, make sure that person is knowledgeable about muscular-skeletal structure and is willing to collaborate with you and the other pain management team members.

11. Review your patients' X-rays and MRI reports with them and discuss how the results impact their choice of the best ways to reduce their chronic pain. Have your patients collaborate with you and other pain management team members to hear their perspectives and conclusions after reading these reports.

12. Encourage your patients to maintain a healthy body weight range. Obesity is a major cause of pain in the whole body and has become a major epidemic in the US. If your patients are overweight, they are at further risk for sleep apnea, diabetes, and high cholesterol and triglyceride levels. Have them see a nutritionist on a regular basis to establish and maintain a healthy eating plan. Have them make an appointment with a nutritionist to determine what should be included in their meal plan, then have them meet regularly with the nutritionist to monitor their food intake. Another option is a weight clinic or, if necessary, a referral for bariatric surgery if all other options haven't worked.

13. Recommend that your patients eat nutritiously. If overweight, they should lose weight and maintain their weight within a healthy weight range over time. Have them watch their calorie intake daily and have them avoid ingesting too many synthetic sugars and artificial sweeteners. Recommend that they eat more fish and chicken and less meat. Also suggest that they include more vegetables and natural sweeteners like fruits in their diets. Have them avoid using saturated fats, and advise them to pay attention to food labels. Suggest they stay away from high-calorie sweets and snacks. Instead, recommend that they eat natural snacks like carrot sticks, celery and nuts. Even air-popped popcorn is a good choice.

14. Your patients should not turn to smoking as an alternative to losing and maintaining their healthy body weight. That's simply exchanging one bad habit for another. Have them consider more adaptive, healthy strategies to cope with "letting go" or mourning the loss of eating unhealthy foods. If necessary, recommend that they see a tobacco cessation specialist or consider hypnosis.

15. Your patients can benefit from a daily structure for building endurance and mobility, improving posture, stretching, muscle strengthening, and whatever exercises you'd suggest based on your assessment of their individual conditions. Getting into a routine is best because they'll feel more hopeful and they'll see positive results if they stick with it.

16. Encourage your patients to exercise, even if it means walking just for a block or two at a time, followed by a rest, even if they need a cane or a walker, and then have them walk again. Walking may seem too boring for them if they were formerly athletic, but it may be the best exercise for them at this time. Have them set realistic sub-goals in walking. Suggest they start out walking a few blocks, then a quarter of a mile, then a half-mile, and have them build up the distance they can handle over time. If they have access to a pool year-round, then they can do their walking in the water. While doing so, they can use foam barbells or waterproof ankle weights to help strengthen their muscles.

17. Prescribe endorphins! Not opiates! You know that your patients have natural opiates that can be much more enjoyable and calming than any prescribed medication. What better "high" is there than aerobic exercise? As a former consistent jogger and as someone who still loves to ride the indoor bicycle (doing different virtual trails while listening to music) and swim, I know what it's like to feel that blood rushing to all your extremities while you relax afterwards, drinking water. Make sure your patients meet with you or a member of their pain management team to determine their optimal heart rate during aerobic activity, and learn how to measure that before, during and after exercise. Stress that it is very important for them to warm up before aerobic exercise, and then cool down after exercising for a realistic (for their physical condition) amount of time. Help your patients establish realistic S.M.A.R.T sub-goals so that they don't magnify their self-expectations. For example, don't have them expect to run a 2-minute mile if they haven't been able to walk up their stairs without getting winded.

    Your patients can choose from a variety of aerobic exercise activities, including power walking, swimming, biking or jogging. There is even aerobic exercise equipment for upper- or lower-body conditioning if your patients have certain pain conditions in either section.

    Getting aerobic exercise is best accomplished if your patients have group support. Having even one or two friends to help them sustain their weekly exercise routine is critical. An alternative is for your patients to commit to a group exercise program like water aerobics, Zumba, or a spinning class.

18. Have your patients choose the right footwear for exercising. Make sure they're wearing comfortable walking or running shoes with excellent support, "bounce" and comfort. If they're not sure about what shoes to purchase, then recommend they see a podiatrist to assess their feet, gait and posture. They may need a specific type of shoe or an orthotic sole to insert in whatever shoe they wear.

19. Suggest that your patients alternate between applying moist heat and ice on their painful areas. Help them find the best "fit" for their physical pain.

20. Suggest that your patients listen to music as they do their daily physical routines. Music soothes the soul and provides much inspiration to help them remain persistent and hopeful.

21. Have your patients drink plenty of water! Have them drink at least sixty-four (64) fluid ounces or eight (8) eight-ounce bottles of water daily.

22. Review their physical pain rating scales on a periodic basis or whenever possible, depending on your time, to spot particular patterns and to help them identify what they are doing that works to reduce their physical pain levels.

23. Have them set new goals. If they find that their sub-goals are too difficult to achieve, then help them divide their sub-goals into several smaller ones. The key is for them to not give up simply because they're frustrated because they can't do what they'd like to be doing. Have them lower their standards if needed, based on their body's signals.

I hope these strategies to reduce your patients' physical pain are as helpful to them as they've been to me. Most of these strategies are based on my professional experience working with people just like them. Others are based on my own personal experiences, having had chronic pain since that traumatic day in August 2008. Remember! What works for one patient to reduce their physical pain will be different from what works for other patients who experience chronic pain.

Try not to sweat the little things.

Chapter 9: Ways to Reduce Your Patients' Pain from Life Stressors

"There is more to life than increasing its speed."
- Mahatma Gandhi

*"Our anxiety does not come from thinking about the future,
but from wanting to control it."*
- Kahlil Gibran

As we've explained throughout this book, chronic pain is not just physical; it can be influenced by life stressors. Some of the ways for your patients to reduce their life stressors may be more difficult than others because they may not have much control over whether certain stressors happen. For example, your patients can't control aging forever, or prevent children from growing up and leaving home, or avoid having to move because of a job loss, or prevent experiencing a traumatic event. Still, your patients can try their best to reduce their chronic pain by choosing some of the following strategies that will help them cope better with life stressors.

1. Encourage your patients to perceive each life stressor as a challenge or an opportunity to grow from confronting it and taking action, rather than catastrophizing (thinking nothing will change or that it's hopeless). Have them maintain their hope even if it takes weeks, perhaps months, to change.

2. Help your patients prioritize all of their life stressors that rank higher than a 7 on the Life Stress Pain Scale. Then have them start with the most important stressors to reduce, and have them work their way down the list.

3. Have your patients clarify whether each high-scaled life stressor is a crisis that may have a significant impact on their pain levels in the immediate future. If it is, they need to work fast to deal with such a stressor head-on, since time becomes a critical factor. If not, then they can still follow the strategies below, but they should focus less on the need for immediate change and more on strategic planning.

4. Recommend that your patients use meditation and relaxation skills while trying to reduce their life stressors. Intermittent breaks in life to relax, de-stress and regroup are important for refueling, so they can deal effectively with their life stressors.

5. Empower your patients to think of how they've coped well with similar stressors in the past. Which strategies worked well? Can they apply similar strategies to the stressors they face now?

6. What information do your patients need to obtain to help them figure out a clear plan to reduce these stressors? Having more knowledge about dealing with their life stressors can help them feel more in control of them. Have your patients gather as much information as they can to handle whatever comes their way.

7. Have your patients consider establishing sub-goals for specific time periods. For example, what can they accomplish today to help them reduce these life stressors? How about in a week? A month? Six months? A year?

8. Encourage your patients to build a network of support. Who or what systems can they rely on to help them cope with life stressors?

9. Recommend that your patients delegate responsibilities as a way of coping with their life stressors. They have nothing to lose by making requests. They'll find that most people are willing to help when they know someone is confronting major stressors in his or her life.

10. What aspects of your patients' life stressors can they control, and what aspects are beyond their control? It's easier to think of plans for the ones they can control. Have them develop and rehearse self-coaching statements and positive rationalizations to deal with those aspects of their life stressors they cannot control.

11. Help your patients focus on using their assertiveness skills. They have the rights to say "No," to make requests, to state their opinions, to express their feelings, to disagree, and to do only what they are humanly capable of doing.

12. Have your patients monitor how well they are doing on reducing their life stressors by using the Life Stress Pain Scale on a regular basis if you have the time.

13. Educate your patients about the common symptoms most people experience when confronting a traumatic event. These include physical, thinking and emotional symptoms indicated by the DSM-5- (*Diagnostic and Statistical Manual of Mental Disorders*) of the American Psychiatric Association.

14. If a patient becomes upset about a life stressor, it will increase their pain. Have your patients try to do whatever it takes to get their life stress levels down to a range of 1 to 4 on the Life Stress Pain Scale by doing mindfulness exercises, using self-calming statements, tapping into visual imagery of peaceful scenes, or taking periodic breaks.

15. If your patients are experiencing a lot of tension between themselves and significant others about resolving major life

stressors, then I would suggest that they try to resolve their conflicts by meeting in a controlled environment, like a food court or some other public place where there are many people around. They may feel more comfortable trying to think of ways to resolve their conflicts without shouting or yelling at one another.

16. If your patients are experiencing much tension about major life stressors, they shouldn't involve their children or teenagers in their discussions with their significant others. Children will experience further stress if they hear your patients having intense arguments. While children need to appreciate that conflicts over life stressors can be resolved in healthy ways, they don't need to get involved in them.

17. Recommend that your patients do not try to get other people who are not involved in the conflict to agree with them. It is not fair to have uninvolved parties take sides.

18. If your patients still cannot resolve their conflicts over major life stressors, then they should get help from a therapist or a mediator who specializes in couples therapy or conflict resolution.

19. Empower your patients to remember that just because they are unable to change a particular life stressor, it doesn't mean they will always feel helpless or be a helpless person.

20. Your patients may not be the pilot of their planes, but they can trust that the Pilot (G-d or a higher power) will get them through their turbulence. What they can do as the navigator is take control of the dials on the instrument panels (the five pain scales) that help strengthen their planes' capacity to navigate them through their storms.

In the next chapter, we'll focus on ways to help your patients reduce their emotional components of chronic pain.

Down goes Pain! Down goes Pain!

Chapter 10: Ways to Reduce Your Patients' Emotional Pain

"I don't want to be at the mercy of my emotions.
I want to use them, to enjoy them, and to dominate them."
- Oscar Wilde

"One thing you can't hide - is when you're crippled inside."
- John Lennon

Beyond physical causes and life stressors, pain can also have an emotional component. There are different categories of emotional pain, and this chapter provides suggestions for handling and reducing these. All the strategies identified in this chapter are based on my professional and personal experiences. Help your patients choose the ones that they find work best for them.

Fight Depression
Nearly everyone experiences different levels of depression and other emotions, even on a day-to-day basis. Just because your patients feel depressed (a rating between 7 and 10 on the Emotional Pain Scale) today doesn't mean

that they'll feel that way every day. So, be aware of when they experience all-or-nothing thinking that they express with statements like, "I'm always depressed." Rather, have them focus on all the days they weren't depressed but simply felt sad or disappointed or, more importantly, encourage them to focus on the days when they feel happy and optimistic.

If, however, they are rating their feelings of depression between a 7 and a 10 almost on a daily basis, their emotional pain level is severe and it implies that they are very depressed and in need of immediate help. They probably feel hopeless and helpless. They need to talk to a mental health professional immediately if they are having any thoughts or specific plans of harming themselves or someone else. Have a person close to them drive them to the nearest hospital emergency room. They will be evaluated by an on-call clinician to determine whether they need to be admitted to a psychiatric inpatient unit for their own safety. Most units are typically short-term with a team that does a diagnostic evaluation, manages medication, and facilitates goal-setting and coping skills groups. This is typically followed on discharge by a partial day treatment program, then intensive outpatient therapy.

Consider getting your patients on medication that helps them with depression. This may be a selective serotonin reuptake inhibitor (SSRI) like fluoxetine (Prozac), sertraline (Zoloft), citalopram (Celexa) or escitalopram (Lexapro); a selective serotonin norepinephrine reuptake inhibitor (SSNRI) like duloxetine (Cymbalta) or venlafaxine HCL (Effexor); or a medicine like bupropion (Wellbutrin) or a tricyclic antidepressant (TCA) like amitriptyline HCL (Elavil). Some of these medications can also help with pain and anxiety. Mood stabilizers like lithium carbonate (Lithobed) or valproic acid (Depakote) may be prescribed for more severe mood disorder conditions like bipolar disorder. Often, newer antipsychotics or anti-convulsant medications can have a positive effect on mood stability. In this category are medications like lamitrogine (Lamictal), aripiprazole (Abilify), respiridone (Respridol) or quetiapine (Seroquel). Other medications like Neurontin or Lyrica can help ease neuropathic pain.

Help your patients look at their daily activity schedule for the week. If they find that they have many unscheduled activities or have planned activities that give them little in the way of feeling mastery and/or pleasure, chances are that this is contributing greatly to their high ratings of depression. Consequently, have them plan more masterful or pleasurable activities into their schedules.

Make sure your patients pay close attention to the specific life stressors that are getting them down. Encourage them to do whatever it takes to lower their stressors by implementing adaptive coping strategies, like implementing S.M.A.R.T. goals with time frames, using positive self-talk and establishing better support systems.

Be aware of whether your patients are self-medicating (i.e., using various substances to dull physical, life stress, emotional pain), and instead, have them try to ease their difficulties by using fortitude skills. It is very common for your patients to have a dual or triple diagnosis of pain, mood disorders, and substance abuse disorders. As mentioned earlier in this book, patients who commit suicide using substances usually do so with a combination of an antidepressant and alcohol.

Recommend that your patients focus on their negative thoughts, then transform them into rational thoughts to reduce their depressive feelings. Have them review the list in Chapter 12 of common negative thoughts that increase depressive conditions and have them use the recommended thought record (similar to the one created by Aaron Beck) to write down their rational thoughts to improve their mood.

Have your patients use thought stopping and distractions to counter the negative thoughts that fuel depression. Have them simply say to themselves, "Stop it!" or have a symbol like a red dot or a stop sign to help them to remember.

Have your patients think of all the ways their situations could be worse -- unless they think like this too much, as that could mean they're more anxious than relieved.

Many occupational therapists recommend that depressed patients try using a weighted blanket when sleeping. The feeling of a heavy, comforting blanket has been shown to be quite effective for reducing depression in patients. Another option may be a lightweight but warm down comforter.

Make sure your patients have an effective support system in place. It may be best to include other people in their lives, like family, friends, or people in their community, rather than simply relying on their caretakers, who can burn out easily.

Control Anxiety

Rating a moderate level of anxiety (ratings of 4 to 6) on the Emotional Pain Scale is a healthy range for most of your patients. Having some level of anxiety can help them initiate action when solving problems or making healthy choices. Too little anxiety (ratings of 1 to 3) can mean that your patients may be unaware of situations that could be unhealthy or dangerous and on which they need to take some kind of action. Having too little anxiety can lead them to act before thinking about the consequences of their actions. The opposite situation can also be a problem. Having too much anxiety can mean that your patients are experiencing some kind of anxiety disorder. High levels of anxiety can increase their muscle tension and blood pressure or deregulate their sugar or cortisol levels.

Find out whether your patients have a genetic predisposition to anxiety disorders in their extended families. Do they or their relatives suffer from some form of generalized anxiety, including constant futuristic, catastrophic worry or possible symptoms like restlessness, sweatiness, light-headedness, or a choking sensation? It's possible for some of them to have panic attacks that last anywhere from a few minutes to hours and come on randomly. There's also agoraphobia, a fear of open places, and a tendency to avoid leaving "secure" places like their homes. Obsessive-compulsive symptoms include thoughts or urges that patients know are silly but believe they must think or act on repetitively. If this sounds like any of your patients' situations, then they may need to be on medications that have been shown to be helpful for long-term anxiety. As well, your patient could benefit from behavioral, therapeutic techniques like response inhibition, exposure, and thought stopping.

Like depressive symptoms, your patients' anxiety symptoms can be masked by the use of substances like alcohol or drugs. Patients often self-medicate, especially since the medical community is cutting back on the prescription and distribution of benzodiazepines like diazepam (Valium), lorazepam (Ativan) or alprazolam (Xanax) because of the potential for your patients to become dependent on them. As well, it is critical that your patients not be prescribed any benzodiazepines if they are taking an opioid medication, even short-term. Try to have your patients be open with you and others affiliated with their pain management team about what they are taking. Still, it may be best to require that they take periodic drug tests to make sure they are not mixing any other drugs that are not being prescribed. This works best if your patient has agreed to sign a medication contract with you or the prescriber on the pain management team. The agreement should spell out positive and negative consequences for medication adherence and should be documented in the patient's electronic health record.

Encourage your patients to learn how to relax. Have them learn breathing and mindfulness techniques practiced in yoga, when doing tai chi, or when listening to relaxation strategies shared on certain applications, podcasts or CDs that teach people how to focus on reducing muscle tension in their bodies. One such practice is the body scan: patients learn to relax each muscle in their body, starting from their feet, through their legs, hips, chest, arms and hands until they reach their heads. Another technique is for them to simply notice any areas in their bodies where they feel tension, then try to focus on relaxing that particular area. Patients should practice doing this in a quiet place for at least ten minutes.

Another relaxation strategy is to simply find or imagine relaxing, peaceful scenes or focus on a monotone sound (like the hum of a fan) or watch a candle glow. The key is for patients to avoid thinking or judging, and instead use their senses to become aware of their surroundings and to generate more alpha, or meditative, brainwave states.

Have them practice the mindfulness strategies recommended in Chapter 12.

Distraction is a critical component in reducing anxiety. Help your patients learn to do something to take their minds away from troubling or negative thoughts and physical symptoms by focusing on something outside themselves.

Encourage your patients to practice a hobby like playing a musical instrument, enjoying a game of cards or doing a crossword puzzle. They can also color, crochet, knit or bird-watch. Have them take an interest in others instead of over-focusing on their own pain.

The strategy of thought stopping (catching themselves having anxious thoughts) is a useful technique for helping patients reduce their negative thoughts. Try having patients use a counting device to count the number of times they have anxious thoughts within certain time periods. Then help them try to reduce that number over time, but be sure they set realistic incremental sub-goals.

Have your patients review the common negative thinking errors (described in the next chapter) that increase anxiety states. Recommend that they use the strategies identified to first catch themselves engaging in these thinking errors, and then have them generate rational responses that will help them to reduce their anxiety.

Help your patients learn to accept that feeling helpless about certain situations at times does not imply that they're a helpless person, and that feeling vulnerable does not mean they're inadequate. The excessive need for control of every situation, and often everyone, is a common negative thought related to anxiety disorders. Those patients who have an excessive need for control can develop panic attacks, an obsessive-compulsive disorder or agoraphobia.

Even obsessive worry can reflect a person's magical belief that, somehow, the more they obsess, the greater is their capacity to control the future. Now, this is different from gathering as much information as possible about an uncertain situation to help problem-solve effectively. Even so, there is a point where one may need to say, "I know enough," given that future predictions are based on probabilities, not certainties.

Just imagine how much pain would be reduced if your patients can accept that not having control of every situation or person is a function of being human, not a sign of weakness.

Cool Anger

Becoming and remaining angry is counterproductive to your patients' efforts to reduce pain. If anything, remaining angry can increase their physical pain and can push others away. Their anger can be a defense against acknowledging other, more vulnerable feelings such as feeling frustrated, ungratified, hurt, rejected, betrayed, unloved, vulnerable, betrayed, helpless, powerless, violated, or misunderstood. In other words, your patients' anger is simply a defense against their feeling "pained."

Help your patients let go of their anger. As a psychologist, I've witnessed hundreds of patients struggling with physical pain that is being aggravated by these underlying feelings. I've been there, as well. Anger only makes one's physical pain worse. Your patients' anger will only increase their physical pain! If they can get in touch with these underlying feelings, then they can let their anger go! Encourage them to share their underlying feelings with their loved ones or with others they can trust to understand what they are truly feeling. If they can do this, they will see their level of physical pain miraculously diminished!

Have your patients try to use these other suggestions to help reduce their anger ratings (on the Emotional Pain Scale) over time.

Have them learn to cool down! If they feel like they're getting too hot and they will react emotionally, then it's clear they've got to cool down quickly before they say or do things they'll regret later.

How do their bodies signal that they are feeling like they are ready to say or do something they may regret? Help your patients recognize the physical signals that especially increase their desire to shout, scream, yell, hit, or throw something.

Have your patients try any of the following to cool down:
- Deep breathing, focusing on each inhale and exhale and counting slowly from 1 to 10, saying the next consecutive number with each exhale.
- Saying to themselves, "Cool down," "Chill," or "Stay calm."
- Take a break. Get away from the scene to calm down and give themselves a chance to think more clearly.

Recommend that your patients be careful that a response of becoming angry is not a result of "mind reading" or projecting their thoughts and feelings onto someone else. This can be a result of their having low self-esteem and thinking, "That person thinks I don't know anything," when it may really mean, "*I* don't think *I* know anything."

If someone becomes angry at your patient, encourage them to respond this way: "What is it about _____ that's making them get so angry?" or "What are other reasons why _____ is becoming angry at me (hurt, pained, misunderstood)?"

Often, anger can result from a misperception, a miscommunication or a distortion. Have your patients reflect on whether any of these conditions may be contributing to their angry feelings.

Review with your patients the medical hazards of becoming angry. From a physical standpoint, getting angry is no different than stomping on the accelerator pedal while a car is in neutral. That's because anger quickly increases the reactions from the sympathetic nervous system, including an increase in blood pressure and heart rate, rapid breathing, muscle constriction, and/or an increase in adrenalin and cortisol levels.

Angry feelings are often a defense against a patient's underlying feelings of pain, helplessness, loss of control, or vulnerability. Have them try to recognize what they're truly feeling instead of simply getting angry.

If your patients' feelings of anger are related to a lack of healthy assertiveness, then have them use the strategies identified in Chapter 12 for improving assertiveness on the Fortitude Scale. Suggest to your patients that becoming angry can push others away. Have them try to use statements like, "I feel hurt when ___" or "I am pained when___." These are more vulnerable feelings to share with someone else, and your patients will notice that others are more willing to listen and respond to what they're thinking and feeling.

Increase Happiness

Most of your patients can learn how to be happy. Martin Seligman, a psychologist and researcher, identified major ways to improve happiness after studying how animals experience "learned helplessness" and become depressed by having no way to avoid pain. Seligman changed his perspective radically to focus on how to improve happiness.
Review the following strategies to improve your patients' happiness.

I suggest you have your patients read the book *Authentic Happiness* by Martin Seligman, the founder of the field of "positive psychology." In his book, Seligman identifies the virtues of happiness and how to obtain and enhance them.

Visit Dr. Seligman's website, wwww.authentichappiness.org, where your patients can do assessments to identify their signature strengths and learn how to develop a positive perspective on how to reduce their chronic pain.

Encourage your patients to smile as much as they can during the day. Have them notice just how much the act of smiling connects them to others and makes them feel better.

Have your patients listen to songs with lyrics that make them feel happy and inspired, or to music that makes them feel good. Every morning, I listen to J.S. Bach, particular Hebrew hymns, show tunes, or my favorite musical artists.

Recommend that your patients listen to their favorite music on a daily basis, especially when they get up in the morning. Encourage them to make a playlist of songs that refer to happiness. Some examples include:

"Don't Worry! Be Happy!"
"Put on a Happy Face"
"Tomorrow"
"The Impossible Dream"
"Climb Every Mountain"
"You'll Never Walk Alone"
"Singing in the Rain"
"Good Vibrations"
"Walking on Sunshine"

Encourage your patients to be happy about the simple things in life. Just the fact that they are able to get up, breathe and use their senses should be enough to make them happy. Help your patients to be happy when they accomplish even small goals in their pain reduction strategies.

Urge your patients to do something kind for someone else at least once weekly. The more they perform acts of kindness for others, the more they will experience happiness and meaningfulness.

Happiness, optimism and gratitude are interrelated. See Chapter 12 for ways to help your patients increase their optimism and gratitude.

Your patients can increase their happiness by simply changing the way they think. In the next chapter, you'll discover ways to help your patients further reduce their pain by changing their ways of thinking.

Sweep away those bad thoughts.

Chapter 11: Ways to Reduce Your Patients' Pain from Negative Cognitive Appraisals

"The tool of thought, and, shaping what he wills,
Brings forth a thousand joys, a thousand ills."
- James Allen, As a Man Thinketh

Research by Aaron Beck and his colleagues has confirmed that there is a strong relationship between how your patients think and how they feel. If they can change their negative thinking, they will change their negative emotional states. This applies to patients' thoughts about their chronic pain.

Have your patients utilize the automatic thought record on pages 139 and 140 to keep a journal of ways to change their negative thinking. In turn, they will see a positive change in their pain levels.

First, have your patients note the date and time of their experience in column one. Next, have them describe the situation in column two. In column three, have your patients note how strongly they are feeling something or their change in physical symptoms on a percentage scale of 0-100, with 0 meaning they have no feeling or physical changes and 100 meaning they feel or experience physical changes strongly. In the fourth column, have your patients identify their automatic thoughts and their relationship to emotional and physical changes, writing down their automatic negative thought(s) on the situation. In column five, have your patients identify what common negative appraisals (listed below in numbered items 1 through 13) are associated with their negative thought(s). Have them use the relevant questions associated with the common negative thoughts to write down a rational response to the same situation in column six. Note how much your patients believe their rational response to be true. Finally, have your patients re-rate their feeling and physical states, using the same percentage scale from 0-100. What differences do they notice in their pain levels if they have a rational response to the same situation?

Let's turn now to thirteen different ways to reduce your patients' pain from having negative thoughts.

1. All-or-Nothing (Dichotomous) Thinking: Have your patients ask themselves these questions: Am I thinking in all-or-nothing ways? Do I see that there is a grey area? How realistic is it to think this way based on the evidence? How probable is it that things will turn out the way I am thinking?

2. Overgeneralization: How realistic is my conclusion? Is it based on objectivity? Evidence? Have there been times in the past when positive experiences occurred that were the opposite of my conclusion? Are there activities I still can do that go against my conclusion? How is it that my overall self-worth is measured by one mistake or by my not meeting one goal?

3. Mental Filtering: Am I filtering in only negative information that fits my assumption? How objective, reliable or valid is this? Are there other possible, positive conclusions I can come to instead of a negative one? Does one bad apple really spoil the whole bunch?

4. Disqualifying the Positive: Why emphasize the negatives? What have been my achievements, however small, rather than my limitations? Is it possible to lower my self-standards? After all, I am human!

AUTOMATIC THOUGHT RECORD

Date/ Time	Describe Stressful Situation Where? With whom? What were you doing?	Emotional/ Physical change 0-100%	Automatic negative thought(s) (How much do you believe it (them) to be true? 0-100%

What is the cognitive appraisal to each negative, automatic thought?	Rational response(s) - Use adapative questions to compose alternative rational response(s) to the stressful situation.	1. How much do you believe the rational response(s) to be true? 0-100% 2. Emotional/Physical change 0-100%

Adapted by the author from materials by Aaron Beck, MD

5. Futuristic Thinking (Jumping to Conclusions): How probable is it that what I am concerned about will occur? What does the history of similar situations tell me? Is it just as likely to be a positive outcome? So what if it turns out negative? Then what? How much control do I really have over determining how it will be? Is it impossible to simply not know? To what extent does thinking about the future take me away from thinking about each moment in time? Can I be mindful of each moment, using my senses without judgment?

6. Catastrophizing (Magnification): How probable is it that my imagined catastrophe is likely to happen? Is there an equally probable positive outcome? What do my past experiences show? How much control do I really have to determine the future? What are the consequences of thinking about the worst-case scenario?

7. Emotional Reasoning: Am I being rational, logical, objective, realistic? Have there been times when I felt something to be true and it turned out to be incorrect?

8. "Should" Statements: Is this thought based on a realistic, rather than an idealistic, self-standard? Is it possible to lower my self-standards to some degree? Do I have a healthy balance between "shoulds" and "loves" or "desires"? Is the "should" based on knowing that I am doing "enough"? In what ways do "should" statements impact my self-esteem?

9. Labeling: What is the evidence to conclude that I should be judging myself in such a harsh manner? Why am I my own worst enemy? Do others perceive me to be this way?

10. Need for Control: How much control do I really have over everything in life? Are there alternative, realistic reasons why I don't have control over this situation? How human is it to feel helpless at times? Just because I feel helpless now, does it mean I'll always feel helpless (all-or-nothing thinking) or that I'm inadequate (labeling)?

11 Personalization: How much responsibility do I really have for something? What are alternative explanations that have nothing to do with me? What is the evidence to prove otherwise? What is the rationale for being so hard on myself?

12. Underestimating Strengths: Why am I only focusing on my vulnerabilities and not on my strengths? What skills or abilities did I possess before that allowed me to have coped well in similar situations?

13. Mind Reading: Is it possible that what I think the other person is thinking or feeling about me isn't accurate? Can they be thinking things other than what I believe has to do with me? To what extent am I projecting my thoughts onto the other person?

You've now had an opportunity to see how, by improving their thinking, your patients can change how they feel and, in turn, decrease their pain. At this point, we will turn to the last section of the book, which focuses on improving your patient's fortitude or their courage to handle pain.

Be more like David, and defeat Goliath.

Chapter 12: Ways to Reduce Your Patients' Pain by Improving Fortitude Skills

"Patience and fortitude conquer all things."
- Ralph Waldo Emerson

"Out of suffering comes the serious mind;
Out of salvation the grateful heart;
Out of endurance, fortitude;
Out of deliverance, faith;
Patient endurance attends to all things."
- Teresa of Avila

Your patients will reduce their pain by increasing their ability to endure hardships. Their ability to perceive their pain as a challenge, rather than a hardship, will transform how they handle it. Once your patients improve their ratings on the seventeen fortitude skills covered in this chapter, they will realize that their pain can be overcome, and that they can decrease adversity.

Explore each of the seventeen skills and then have your patients determine which strategies they will use to transform the ways they can handle pain into pursuing a positive Pain Management Lifestyle.

Seventeen Skills for Your Fortitude Tool Kit

Coping Skills	Cognitive Flexibility
Self-Care	Optimism
Self-Efficacy	Humor
Assertiveness	Resilience
Exercise	Gratitude
Distraction	Supportive Systems
Mindfulness	Love
Problem-Solving	Spirituality
Self-Monitoring	

Coping Skills

*"In three words I can sum up everything I've
learned about life. It goes on."*
- Robert Frost

Your patient's ability to confront their upsets and disappointments is a critical factor in reducing their chronic pain. It's become harder these days since the rapid advancements in technology have contributed to people wanting things immediately. Faster is not necessarily better. Improving your patients' coping skills is simply the ability to have them refine the skills they've learned (hopefully) in childhood. Invite your patients to choose from the following strategies the ones that work best for them.

1. Have your patients reflect on adaptive ways they've dealt with their frustrations and disappointments related to experiencing chronic pain in their past.

2. Have your patients reflect on positive role models they've either encountered personally or heard or read about over time. Encourage them to reflect on the adaptive ways these people coped well with upsetting situations, especially chronic pain. What skills or abilities did they have? What did these role models value that helped them earn your patient's respect?

3. Encourage your patients to write down and rehearse positive, inspirational quotes or song lyrics, or have them read stories that reflect positive virtues about how to handle upsets, especially when it concerns coping with pain.

4. Suggest that your patients create their day each morning by thinking about, then writing down, how they're going to be. For example, they can write down "Be positive all day" or "Cope well with my pain" or "Be patient with _____." They'll be surprised by how creating their day this way, and starting their statements with the word "be," will help them feel more positive about life.

5. Encourage your patients to smile all day. Have them smile and say hello to as many of the people they meet as they can.

6. Have your patients prepare in advance for potential cognitive, emotional or physical triggers that can induce them to not cope well. Have them develop and keep strategic plans in place should they encounter such triggers.

7. Encourage your patients to rehearse how they will cope adaptively to these triggers. Have them write down a sufficient number of "if-then" scenarios they may encounter.

8. Tell your patients to not react! Suggest that they first calm down! Have them take a time-out, a quick break or even retreat if they can. Then, have them think the situation through before they decide on which coping strategies to use. Suggest that they use diaphragmatic (deep) breathing or do a mindfulness exercise first.

9. Encourage your patients to use their support network. This could be anyone they can call, text, or email, especially if they're feeling vulnerable to not coping well with their pain.

10. Empower your patients be their own best coach when it comes to coping with chronic pain.

11. Recommend that your patients use higher-level coping strategies like sublimation and humor. Have them write in a journal or

create poems, write short stories, song lyrics, fiction or non-fiction books. Suggest that they draw, paint, color, sing, play an instrument, or listen to music. Encourage them to attend concerts and plays or watch comedies, old and new. Have them read or listen to books, especially biographies of people who have endured pain.

12. Have your patients remember that their situation could be a lot worse compared to situations others are facing.

13. Encourage your patients to rehearse and use daily positive self-coping statements like the following:

- "Be brave and carry on despite the pain."
- "I can overcome the pain."
- "I won't let my pain stand in the way of what I want to do."
- "I can handle this."
- "Stay relaxed."
- "Live one moment at a time."
- "Never give up."

14. Try to get your patients to rehearse and use daily words of inspiration like the following:

- "Success is the sum of small efforts, repeated day in and day out." Robert Collier
- "To climb steep hills requires a slow pace at first." William Shakespeare
- "While there is life, there is hope." Cicero
- "Hope is a waking dream." Aristotle
- "Never lose hope." Unknown
- "Pain happens but suffering is optional." Unknown

Self-Care

"Until you value yourself, you won't value your time. Until you value your time, you will not do anything with it."
- M. Scott Peck

Self-care is a key component of self-esteem. Here are some ways to help your patients improve their self-esteem and thus improve their fortitude skills.

1. Have your patients take a sheet of paper and divide it into two parts. On the left side, have them make a list of things they have to do. On the right side, have them list the things they'd love to do or have passion for doing. Now, have them rate the importance of each item from 1 to 5, with 1 being "not very important" and 5 being "very important." Encourage them to focus on developing a commitment to activities on the right side of their sheet that is just as strong as their commitment to activities on the left side. Have them try to balance the sheet as much as possible.

2. Don't let your patients' rationalizations become obstacles that keep them from doing things they'd love to do, as long as they're objectively realistic, timely and cost-effective.

3. Encourage your patients to reaffirm their commitment with statements like, "I deserve to do _____" or "I work hard enough to enjoy _____."

4. Recommend that your patients generate a good support system to help themselves begin and continue self-care activities.

5. Try to get your patients to be wary of all-or-nothing thinking or labeling. Just because they care for themselves doesn't mean they're "selfish" or never caring for others. Even cars need refueling to keep going, and your patients are no different.

6. If your patients are not used to initiating self-care activities, then have them get their feet wet a little at a time. Encourage them to do certain activities for short time periods or try activities that won't make them feel too guilty about taking time for themselves. Then have them begin to increase these activities

over time so that they find a healthy balance between self-care activities and those that give them a sense of mastery or self-efficacy.

7. If your patients tend to be perfectionists, then help them transform the use of the word "should." Encourage them to say things like, "I should relax!" or "I should care for myself" or "I should reward myself by doing something nice for myself after doing some must-do task!"

Self-Efficacy

Self-efficacy is the extent to which your patients derive satisfaction from accomplishing things. These things can range from completing small projects around their homes or writing poems to making regular donations of time or needed items at a local food pantry or animal shelter.

1. Help your patients realize their skills or abilities (every one of us has many) rather than telling themselves that they have none. Encourage them to review their lists of common skills or abilities, then have them rate themselves on each skill from 1 to 5, with 5 meaning they definitely have this skill and 1 meaning they definitely don't have this skill. A good starter list of skills can be found in *What Color Is Your Parachute?* (2017) by Richard Bolles.

2. Encourage your patients to do those activities that give them a sense of accomplishment and satisfaction. Have them rate those activities on a scale of 1-5 (with 1 indicating little sense of accomplishment and 5 indicating a strong feeling of accomplishment), and then have them schedule more activities that they can rate as higher than a 3.

3. Make sure the activities your patients identify are realistic and definable. If not, then suggest that they break down their activity goals into sub-goals.

4. Encourage your patients to be proud of their accomplishments. Recommend that they reward themselves with a self-care activity after they complete each self-efficacy activity; even if it's a sub-goal.

5. Have your patients learn about their pain. Knowledge helps them to be more in control of their pain. There is always more to learn, but don't recommend that they become stuck with the cognitive error of "I don't know enough." That will only make them feel inadequate and anxious, especially if they're perfectionistic. Instead, suggest that they learn as much as they can while realizing learning is an ongoing process through life. Encourage them to focus on what they *do* know instead of on what they don't know.

6. The more your patients do things for satisfaction and accomplishment, the higher will be their level of confidence and their ratings on resilience on the Fortitude Scale.

Assertiveness
"Too many of us fail to fulfill our needs because we say no rather than yes, yes when we should say no."
-William Glasser

Assertiveness is another way to increase your patients' fortitude. Their ability to say what they think, to change their minds, and say, "No" will help them build confidence and lower their pain.

Helping those patients who experienced trauma from wartime or physical or sexual abuse to learn to be more assertive can be empowering for you. The same is true for helping patients who internalize their anger, and have the potential to increase somatic conditions, to express themselves in a more forthright manner.

For example, I've seen many patients diagnosed with fibromyalgia who have high levels of "helpless rage." This could be from situations in which they felt intensely frustrated and had no control, like being in previous traumatic situations, or being victims of abuse in more recent situations. Learning to be more assertive can have an amazing impact on their pain levels.

Help your patients recognize that their rights include the following; credit for items 1 through 10 goes to Manuel J. Smith.

1. The right to judge their own behavior, thoughts, and emotions, and to take responsibility for their initiation and consequences upon themselves.

2. The right to offer no reasons or excuses for justifying their behavior.
3. The right to judge if they are responsible for finding solutions to other people's problems.
4. The right to change their minds.
5. The right to make mistakes and be responsible for them.
6. The right to say, "I don't know."
7. The right to be independent of the goodwill of others before coping with them.
8. The right to be illogical in making decisions.
9. The right to say, "I don't understand."
10. The right to say, "I don't care."
11. The right to say what they think.
12. The right to say, "No!"
13. The right to say that "It is not realistic."
14. The right to say how they feel.
15. The right to disagree.
16. The right to make requests.
17. The right to not tolerate any kind of abuse.
18. The right to care for themselves.
19. The right to be treated with respect.
20. The right to feel good about themselves.
21. The right to be in trusting relationships.
22. The right to feel good.
23. The right to feel helpless at times.

Recommend that your patients keep an assertiveness journal. Have them identify the date and time of the situation, including who or what was involved and what your patients heard, saw or read, which of the above rights was being violated, how they responded, and what the consequences were. Most important is helping them to create adaptive assertiveness strategies that earn them self-respect and respect from others.

Encourage your patients to assert themselves using the DESC script; DESC is an acronym that stands for Describe, Emote, Specify, Consequence.

1. Describe: Have your patients write down or say what they saw, heard or read as if they are newspaper reporters simply noting the facts. For example, "John, this is the fifth time today that you told me to forget about the pain."

2. Emote: Encourage your patients to express how what they saw, heard or read made them feel. For example, "I feel hurt that you don't seem to appreciate the level of pain I am in."
3. Specify a request. For example, "I'm asking that you stop saying that and be more understanding of what I am going through."
4. Consequence: Have your patients make up an "if-then" statement. For example, "If you stop saying that and support me in an understanding way, then I'll feel closer to you."

Encourage your patients to rehearse potential situations they believe may occur using assertiveness steps described above. If they feel overwhelmed by their feelings in a situation, suggest that they take a time-out to calm down by doing some deep breathing or a mindfulness exercise. Encourage them to practice the DESC script, and then have them return to the situation to assert themselves.

Recommend that your patients take additional time to calm down to think through what they want to say or write.

Strongly suggest that your patients not "take the bait" if they believe their rights are being violated and they believe they are being set up to respond inappropriately or are about to respond ineffectively to a high-stress statement or action by another. Encourage them to think before they respond and re-check what they want to say or write. Have them get a reality check on how they're going to respond by getting feedback from other people. This is especially true with instant messaging, texting, or commenting on social media platforms. Recommend that they try to use cool-down comments or humor to manage any heightened tension.

Exercise
"We are what we repeatedly do. Excellence then is
not an act but a habit."
- Aristotle

"Prescribe endorphins! Not opioids!"
- Dr. George Beilin

There is nothing better than seeing your patients committed to getting exercise and finding a natural high from the release of their bodies' endorphins. If they can swim or ride a stationary bike or even walk for thirty-five minutes, then encourage them to do it! If you've ever been to Positano, a beautiful town along the Amalfi Coast in Italy, you'll know why the people there are so healthy. Why? Because they eat a lot of fish and they walk up and down stairs along mountainous hillsides. I'm convinced that my beloved grandmother, who lived with us until she was 93 years old, sustained her life because she, too, walked up and down our home stairs, from the second floor to the basement and back, every day.

Be mindful of your patients generating all the reasons that can get in the way of exercising. Suggest that they consider these strategies to increase their fortitude:

1. Make sure that they don't give up, no matter what, even if they can do just a little physical activity every day or every few days.

2. Have your patients collaborate with you and members of their pain management team to design a realistic exercise program based on their pain levels and what they can tolerate. Make sure that they have a careful assessment done before beginning any type of exercise. Focus on helping them improve their endurance, stability, mobility, and strength. Most importantly, you want to help them be mindful of any triggers that can induce them to relapse, like generating all kinds of rationalizations to stay at home, become sedentary or even lie in a bed all day long.

3. Suggest that they stretch after they exercise. Again, have them review with you and other members of their pain management team which are the best stretches for them, based on their conditions.

4. Encourage them to set up a daily routine that may include walking in places where they can sit to take frequent breaks as needed.

5. Make sure your patients develop support teams. Have them consider exercising with at least one other person. It's great when your patients can coach each other to exercise. Walking or doing other exercise with a friend makes it seem less strenuous.

Distraction
"All profound distraction opens certain doors."
- Julio Cortazar

Encourage your patients to take time to simply "get away from it all" – it's a healthy way to reduce their pain. Distraction is better than prescribing benzodiazepines to those patients who experience heightened anxiety. Even the best sports coaches know when to call a time-out to have their teams regroup to gain perspective and re-focus. Here are some strategies that your patients may find helpful:

1. Have your patients focus on activities that distract them from becoming preoccupied by negative thoughts, worrying, body symptoms, or withdrawing excessively. These activities could be anything: hobbies, reading, listening to talk shows or music, playing an instrument, taking an interest in someone else, doing good deeds, playing a game or doing a crossword puzzle, watching a movie or a sports event, or taking a course or webinar.

2. Encourage your patients to structure their days so that they can gain both mastery and pleasure from those activities that distract them from their chronic pain.

3. Have them use a mindfulness exercise as described in the next section of this chapter.

Mindfulness
"The present moment is filled with joy and happiness.
If you are attentive, you will see it."
- Thich Nhat Hanh

The term "mindfulness meditation" has been around for centuries. The methodology has simply been reframed, perhaps for marketing purposes. Buddhist monks have practiced the steps over time, like focusing on the present, being still within a peaceful environment, and concentrating on one's breath. Meditation techniques go back even earlier to the practices of Vedanta, Sanskrit (India), Sufi, and Jewish traditions. Since the 1960s, we have had other reframes as, for example, the writings of Suzuki, in *Zen Mind, Beginners Mind* and Baba Ram Das/ Richard Alport's *Be Here Now.* Then came Transcendental Meditation (TM), where individuals paid several hundred dollars simply to get a one-word nonsense syllable of their own to practice saying repeatedly. The practice of Hatha Yoga was much inspired by the Maharishi Yogi and his influence on the Beatles.

All of this is okay. Embrace whatever works for your patients to de-stress and reduce their negative chronic pain scale scores while improving their fortitude scale scores. Just remember that your patients don't necessarily have to pay money to "go somewhere" to learn about how to "be in the present."

For your patients who enjoy reading, I would strongly recommend *The Relaxation Response* by Herbert Benson (1973). I find this to be the best book to help your patients learn the key medical ingredients and benefits of any type of meditational exercise. In his book, Benson reviews the significant impact of meditation on one's physiological condition, including heart-rate, blood pressure, cholesterol and cortisol levels. Several other books for your patients to consider reading are *Peace Is Every Step* by Thich Nhat Hanh (1990), and *Mindfulness for Beginners* (2006) and *Full Catastrophe Living* (1990) by Jon Kabat-Zinn. The latter book is especially helpful because it is based on Zinn's work at the Pain Reduction Program at the University of Massachusetts Medical Center.

Here are the keys to mindfulness meditation:

- Have your patients find a quiet space where they won't be disturbed.
- Have them focus on their sensory awareness -- just using their senses: what they see, hear, smell, taste and touch, moment by moment. One possibility is to have them focus on a constant sound, like the hum of a fan or the ticking of a clock, or on a constant object, like a candle glowing or a spot on a wall.
- Have them do diaphragmatic (deep) breathing or visualization: Have them sit in a chair or lie down in a quiet area. Then have them close their eyes and breathe in, and breathe out, as deeply as they can, saying to themselves "in" or "one" on the in-breath and "out" or "two" on the out-breath. If they prefer visualization, have them imagine the ocean receding from the shoreline or rich, blue-colored air when they inhale, and the waves breaking on the shore or grey-colored air when they exhale.
- Make sure they avoid judgment: Encourage them to stop any kind of thinking, especially judgments. If they find their mind wandering, then suggest that they try to stop it and have them bring themselves back to focusing on their diaphragmatic breathing or on a constant sound or object.

There are other ways for your patients to practice sensory awareness training as a means of meditation to reduce their stress and their chronic pain. For example, recommend that they take pictures or videos spontaneously with their phone cameras. Encourage them to find scenes or objects that appeal to them, then have them walk around snapping pictures or taking videos that capture their senses. Again, suggest that they focus on their senses without any judgement! Another practice is to take a sketchbook and draw something that they observe, perhaps a scenic area. Have them focus on their drawings and enjoy the motions of their hands and the feel of the paper and pencils. Recommend that they try walking in a garden or a greenhouse or near the ocean. Encourage them to focus on their sense of smell. Hiking—even short distances where they can stop at different points to rest—is a great way for them to become fully aware of all their senses.

There are multiple applications and podcasts to help your patients learn and use meditation to calm their minds. Have them find the ones that work best for them.

I strongly recommend that your patients practice mindfulness meditation at least twice daily for a minimum of ten minutes each session. Have them try this: first, rate their levels of physical pain from 1-10. Second, have them practice a mindfulness exercise. Third, have them re-rate their levels of pain to see how much their pain levels have decreased after the exercise.

Problem-Solving Skills

*"A sum can be put right: but only by going back
till you find the error and working it afresh from the point,
never by simply going on."*
- C.S. Lewis

Your patients' ability to problem-solve is a gift that elevates them above all the other animals on this earth. It indicates that they are capable of reasoning and using their memories effectively to analyze problems and resolve them, using the best steps they can think of, to form a conclusion. Encourage your patients to choose from among these strategies to improve their ratings on this element of the Fortitude Scale.

Recommend to your patients that they identify the major problems they are facing, making sure they are not hiding more important problems. Then have them think of all the ways they can deal with their problems, even if they must be patient with the fact that their problems cannot be solved right away. Then, have them weigh the pros and cons of each plan. They can do a cost-benefit analysis of each plan that includes a weighted scale from 1 to 5 for each benefit and cost. Make sure that they think of the benefits and costs of using specific plans, both short- and long-term. Then have them choose the best plans and act on them and evaluate how they did!

Make sure your patients prioritize their problems! Have them place their problems that relate to reducing their chronic pain into four categories:

1) Problems that need to be handled immediately or within the next 24 hours.
2) Problems that they can address within a week or two.
3) Problems that can be put off for a longer period of time.
4) Those problems they can delegate to others.

As they are thinking about how to solve their current problems, have them think of all the positive ways they've successfully handled past problems and reduced their chronic pain. These can range from easy problems to moderately hard to difficult ones. They can be work-related problems, or family or interpersonal problems. What skills did it take for them to solve these problems well?

After they define the problems clearly, then recommend that they identify what information they may need to obtain to help them define some ways to solve their problems. The more information they have, the more control they will have to eventually choose the best plans to reduce their pain.

Sometimes the biggest problem can be that they aren't really clear on what their problems are. For example, the problem can be a misperception, a misunderstanding, or a miscommunication. For example, they may think that the problem is that their spouse doesn't care about their pain; that their spouse is fed up with their acting as if they can't cope. You can help your patient reframe that their spouse is scared that they are acting as if they are giving up and that they don't want to live. In fact, their spouse loves them and doesn't want to lose him/her.

Encourage your patient to use visualization techniques to problem-solve effectively. Have them close their eyes and imagine themselves reaching a positive solution to their problems. Now have them imagine going through all the steps to reach their solution. What steps did they envision going through to reach their positive outcomes?

Make sure that your patients emphasize what they did well when problem-solving. Have your patients become their own supportive, encouraging self-coach, no matter how well they did. The worst-case scenario is that at least they tried!

It is the action that will bring your patients the most satisfaction and/or pleasure. Make sure they just do it! Don't allow them to get stuck on any one step in the sequence of problem-solving actions.

The better your patients are at problem-solving, the higher their resilience ratings on their Fortitude Scales will be -- and that's important for their Pain Management Lifestyle.

Self-Monitoring

"Self-discipline is often disguised as short-term pain, which often leads to long-term gains. The mistake many of us make is the need and want for short-term gains (immediate gratification), which often leads to long-term pain."
- Charles Glass

Your patients need to think before they act! How easy it is to say this when they are being inundated with all kinds of ways to get something done right this second. Even buying items online takes just a push of a phone button rather than a drive to the shopping mall. The number of people becoming phone- and internet-addicted is rising dramatically. It's a blessing for your patients to slow down and weigh their options. It will reduce their pain, as well. Have your patients choose from the following strategies the ones that will work the best for them.

1. Having an "observing self" is key to your patients reducing their chronic pain. From infancy, all of us have developed this inner capacity to talk to ourselves about situations and inner sensations. Your patients learned this from developing the use of their memory and then their use of language to self-monitor their thoughts, feelings and actions. Encourage your patients to listen to their "inner voice" and clarify whether it is helping to guide them to think and reason in adaptive ways. If their inner voice is not helpful in this way, then I'd suggest that your patients re-focus on changing their negative thinking, as measured by the Cognitive Appraisal Scale.

2. It's important to have your patients use all five of the pain rating scales at least once or twice weekly to evaluate how they are doing to reduce their chronic pain. Help them clarify what has helped them and what hasn't helped them to change their ratings

in positive ways. Encourage them to choose better strategies than the ones that aren't working so well.

3. Your patients should emphasize the last segment of problem-solving, asking themselves, "How did I do?" to evaluate what they put into action to reduce their chronic pain. Have them ask, "Did it work or not?"

4. Encourage your patients to not think too much or obsess. Excessive thinking will just make them more worried and anxious. They want to be confident in their evaluations, not preoccupied with doubt and self-criticism. This is especially true if they are perfectionists who have high self-standards. Suggest that they be positive coaches to themselves, not constant critics!

Cognitive Flexibility
"The measure of intelligence is the ability to change."
- Albert Einstein

Your patients are often required to shift from one task to another. This capacity is a major executive function of the brain's prefrontal cortex. Cognitive flexibility or cognitive shifting means that your patients have the ability to change course when meeting upsets or disappointments. They can be cognitively flexible, self-monitor their situations, then problem-solve and renew their coping abilities.

They may have difficulty with this task, especially if they are concentrating deeply on one, then are interrupted to change their focus because they have to do something else. This can be quite difficult if they really like what they are doing and do not expect this sudden change. To reduce your patients' feelings of frustration and pain and to prevent possible arguments with significant people in their lives who may ask them to "stop what you are doing and please help me with _____," I recommend that you encourage them to choose from the following strategies the ones that may best help them increase their fortitude in this area.

1. Instead of allowing your patients to become stuck in grieving their losses, help them accept their pain as a challenge. Encourage them to regain their hope that all is not lost. Suggest that they act in ways to reduce their pain so that their pain

doesn't consume them. Then recommend that they maintain their commitment to the specific pain management strategies they've chosen that prevent relapses. They can always create new sub-goals rather than try to meet overly idealistic ones. If they lose five pounds, then setting another sub-goal of losing five more pounds can be attainable. If a patient is capable of walking a few blocks, then a new goal might be walking a half-mile next time. Their intent to love each moment can be amended to loving life.

2. Make sure your patients realize that they may have periodic upsets that impede their ability to reduce their chronic pain. Having cognitive flexibility means that they can think about and implement ways to overcome any obstacles that keep them from reducing their chronic pain.

3. Have your patients consider generating backup plans if things get in the way of the first plans they put into action.

4. Encourage your patients to manage their anger when experiencing frustrations. Suggest that they use calming techniques to stop and think before they react. Help them learn to be patient, yet assertive.

5. Warn your patients against setting unrealistically high standards, for themselves or for others, especially if they are perfectionistic. Try having them lower their standards and be less hard on themselves.

6. Make sure your patients pay close attention to possibly having high ratings of control on the Cognitive Appraisal of Pain Scale. Have them try to reframe not having control over situations as simply temporary experiences of helplessness that are part of the human condition.

7. Recommend that your patients read the Serenity Prayer often, even if they don't attend Alcoholics Anonymous (AA) or Narcotics Anonymous (NA) meetings. If they don't know it, here it is; your patients may address it to G-d or to any other power they choose: "Grant me the serenity to accept the things I cannot change, courage to change the things I can; and the wisdom to know the difference."

Optimism

"A pessimist sees the difficulty in every opportunity;
The optimist sees every opportunity in every difficulty."
- Winston Churchill

This quote from Winston Churchill best encapsulates the importance of cultivating optimism. Have your patients choose from among the following strategies the ones that may work best for them to improve their optimism ratings on the Fortitude Scale.

1. In his book *Learned Optimism*, Martin Seligman writes about how optimism can be enhanced. Encourage your patients to perceive their problems with chronic pain as being temporary and view them as mostly controllable (or capable of being reduced). The third step is to help your patients understand that they are mostly specific to the situation rather than generalizable to all situations.

2. Optimistic people are happier than those people who think negatively and catastrophize about the future. Try to help your patients to stop their negative thinking by using thought-stopping techniques. Have them pinch themselves or snap a rubber band around their wrists every time they have a negative thought, and have them say to themselves, "Stop it!" Or use visual cues like red dots or have them make a "stop sign" to remind themselves to stop and think.

3. To be optimistic is to have hope in a manner similar to hostages held in captivity for long periods of time. Encourage your patients to do whatever it takes to instill hope, including reading or listening to anything inspirational.

4. Optimistic people let things go. Recommend to your patients that they don't hold onto grudges or upsets with people. Encourage them to apologize and work through as many conflicts as they can. Their experiences of having chronic pain can make them hypersensitive to what others say and do. Make sure they are careful that they don't mind-read, misunderstand or misperceive what is really going on between someone else and themselves.

5. Help your patients to change the way they view obstacles to reducing their chronic pain by having them see obstacles as challenges or opportunities. Their challenges are a function of their life journeys; help patients to think of them as positive ways to transform their negative thoughts, feelings and actions.

6. Encourage your patients to generate a positive probable outcome for every anticipated negative outcome of an action plan to reduce their chronic pain.

7. Encourage your patients to smile as much as possible within themselves and towards others. They'll find that smiling is catchy and fuels positive connectedness with others.

8. Martin Seligman notes that instead of blaming themselves, optimists focus on the notion that factors beyond their control, due to circumstances or to someone else's actions, caused a negative experience. The more you can encourage your patients to do this, the lower their ratings should be on "control" on the Cognitive Appraisal Scale.

Humor
"A day without laughter is a day wasted."
- Charlie Chaplin

In his book *Anatomy of an Illness as Perceived by the Patient*, Norman Cousins describes how ten minutes of laughter daily, as an adjunct to traditional treatment, helped him overcome what doctors believed was a one-in-a-hundred chance of surviving an adrenal disease. Mr. Cousins believed that positive emotions could bring about well-being. In his life, Mr. Cousins used humor to avoid bypass surgery. Asked about these experiences, he said he believed humor was a powerful tool for reducing anxiety, panic, and helplessness.

1. Encourage your patients to recognize the benefits of humor. It improves their immune system functions, lowers their stress levels, and increases their positive outlook on life. Humor can increase their happiness and lower their ratings on depression, anxiety and anger on the Emotional Pain Scale. It can also increase their optimism and resilience ratings on the Fortitude Scale.

2. As much as they can, have your patients avoid reading or listening to any news that increases their anger or despair. Instead, encourage them to watch comedies, listen to funny talk shows, read and listen to jokes, funny stories, and satire. Empower them to laugh at the absurdities of life. Help them try to find jokes about coping with pain. As strange as this may sound, they may find the humor about pain to be a stress reliever.

3. Encourage your patients to look for any opportunity to use humor in conversations. Everyone experiences some form of pain, whether it be due to physical causes, life stress, emotional stages, negative cognitive appraisals or lack of fortitude. None of your patients are exempt from pain. Encourage them to use humor tactfully to help others reduce their life pain.

4. Urge your patients to be around people who have a good sense of humor. It brings them closer together.

5. Help your patients gain the power to laugh at themselves rather than be self-critical. Disparagement theory is about having the ability to laugh at oneself and one's human frailties.

Resilience

"Resilience is accepting your new reality, even if it's less good than the one you had before. You can fight it, you can do nothing but scream about what you've lost, or you can accept that and try to put together something that's good."
- Elizabeth Edwards

Resilience is the ability to grow from painful experiences. The greater your patients' resilience, the more effective they will be in overcoming setbacks and upsets.

1. Encourage your patients to think of times when they were able to bounce back from having chronic pain. What abilities, virtues and strengths did they have that helped them bounce back? To what extent did they acknowledge themselves for having the ability to use these traits again to face future setbacks, should they occur?

2. Have your patients think of others they know who have had chronic pain and have bounced back fairly well. What did they think it took for them to do so?

3. Suggest that your patients ask themselves, "What happens when you've had a setback?" Support them in thinking, "That's okay! Just don't be so hard on yourself! It's no different than having a relapse." It may just be that some of their weekly monitored negative scale ratings may increase or their positive ones may decrease. Encourage your patients to remember that their overall goal of having a Pain Management Lifestyle is to improve their pain scale ratings over time. The essential thing is to try to increase their average number of healthy days or weeks in between setbacks, over time.

4. Help your patients recognize triggers that induce their setbacks. Often, they're related to increased negative thinking or feelings of anxiety, depression or anger. Their triggers may be due to some life stressors beyond their control or they could simply stem from an aggravated physical condition that may require them to seek another medical consult. When they have a setback, have them think about what they need to get back on track to improve their scale ratings. For example, have them note what they can do differently to lower their ratings on the anger and life stress scales and improve their ratings on the resilience scale.

5. Have them make a list of times in their lives when they confronted other challenges and were able to bounce back. These challenges could have been at any age, with family or friends, at school or work, or when they were involved in different organizations. These challenges could have been about their health, a life-stage crisis, or about their finances. After they lost these challenges, ask them what it took for them to bounce back.

6. As mentioned previously, a healthy sleep pattern is important to resilience. If your patients are not getting enough sleep, they need to talk to you or another member of their pain management team about what may help them to sleep more effectively.

7. Recommend that your patients think of ways they can increase meaningfulness in their lives. How can they make a difference, gain satisfaction from helping others or help to promote an important cause?

8. Help your patients do whatever it takes to confront their fears or worries that may make them avoid steps to reduce their chronic pain. Have them review strategies to deal with their negative thinking and excessive worries. If they have fears that relate to taking action to reduce their chronic pain, then make sure that they meet with you or another professional team member who can teach them the relevant muscle relaxation techniques to be paired with a hierarchy of the fears that increase with intensity. This process is called systemic desensitization.

9. Your patients' resilience and optimism are often correlated. That is, the more they maintain a positive outlook, the more resilient they may be. Have them think of some positive words of encouragement they've said to themselves or heard others say that can help them improve their resilience and reduce their chronic pain ratings.

10. Recommend that your patients make a list of their particular strengths and virtues. Have them review the list of the ones noted in the book *Authentic Happiness* (2002) by Martin Seligman.

11. Humor and resilience can often go together. Ask your patients, "To what extent can you use humor to deal with setbacks?" Encourage them to think of times in the past when they were able to get through difficult days using humor.

12. Empower your patients to do simple, enjoyable activities they can build into their day to help them improve their ability to bounce back from situations and to help reduce their chronic pain.

13. Help them identify their support networks of people they can rely on when they must overcome setbacks and improve their resilience.

14. Make sure your patients keep to some sort of routine to help them reduce their chronic pain.

15. Encourage your patients to reframe their capabilities to confront their stress as positive opportunities to grow from challenges.

Gratitude
"Walk as if you are kissing the earth with your feet"
- Thich Nhat Hanh

Your patients' ability to be grateful goes a long way towards offsetting the stresses, strains and worries that can consume their minds. Being grateful helps to make their pain and suffering less of a focus than their happiness and pleasure.

1. Empower your patients to be grateful even for the simplest things. Have them try it out! And they will see how their being grateful each day reduces their chronic pain!

2. Encourage your patients to get up each morning and express gratitude for the positive experiences they have in their lives. Must they wait for Thanksgiving to express gratitude? It's easy for them to focus on their pain, their anger, their hurts, what they could have been, or should have done, rather than the things in their lives that bring them comfort, nurturance and meaningfulness.

3. Your patients can share how much they're grateful when praying, as in thanking G-d or a higher power for the gift of life; for giving them food from this earth; for giving them water to drink, and for giving them clothes to wear.

Expressing gratitude goes a long way towards helping your patients offset the stresses, strains, and worries that can consume their minds.

Being grateful can make their pain and suffering less of a focus than happiness and pleasure—even for the simplest things.

Supportive Systems

"A best friend is the only one that walks into
your life when the world has walked out."
- Shannon L. Alder

Your patients will have much difficulty living alone with their pain. They can cry in agony in bed or, they can choose to have those whom they love understand and help them make better choices to reduce their pain. Having a healthy supportive system of family or coworkers or friends is no different for a chronic pain patient than a patient who is suffering from overeating or from abusing substances. Having people care about your patients' life challenges can be as fruitful as a blossoming spring tree.

Encourage your patients to consider some of the following strategies to improve their supportive systems.

1. Have them write down a list of people, groups or organizations that can help support them in their efforts to reduce their chronic pain. This especially includes others who experience chronic pain and those caretakers who can empathize well with their situations.

2. Your patients can gain support by listening to positive, optimistic information; meeting directly with others or communicating by phone, e-mail or text; joining online supportive networks; attending workshops; or by joining a free support group in their area.

3. One wonderful social media site you can encourage your patients to visit is meetup.com. It's a wonderful place to discover what groups are available within a certain distance from their homes. These groups include a wide range of interests and are especially helpful for your patients to use in finding groups for exercise like walking and biking, for hobbies like art or music, or simply personal support groups.

4. Make sure your patients feel support from you and members of their pain management team. This includes seeing you or a clinician who specializes in pain management, on a regular basis, even if it's just for periodic check-ins.

5. If your patients cannot make a scheduled on-site therapy

appointment, then have them consider tele-health, whereby their insurance companies will pay for them to receive help through a secure online video program. If their insurance companies don't allow this, then I'd suggest you and your pain management team members contact your patients' insurance companies and advocate for them to endorse it.

6. Encourage your patients to participate! Make sure they don't create reasons to avoid connecting with others, especially those who are quite knowledgeable about chronic pain. Your patients are not alone in having chronic pain!

Love
"The capacity to care is the thing that
gives life its deepest significance."
- Pablo Casals

Love is a powerful force in reducing your patients' chronic pain. Encourage them to consider "Emuna," which in Hebrew means an unconditional belief and faith that everything emanates from G-d. To love G-d and to know G-d loves your patients because he created them is a primary way to experience Divine Love. In the Old Testament, it is written, "And you shall love the Lord thy G-d, with all thy heart, with all thy soul and with all thy might." In the New Testament, love emanates from the sayings of Jesus and his disciples. In the Quran, love is derived from one's direct relationship with Allah, based on the writings of the Prophet Mohammed. Recommend that your patients read the sayings of Buddha and Confucius as they apply to love.

If any of these sources are uncomfortable for your patients to believe in, then encourage them to consider having faith in a higher power or spiritual forces like those revered by Native Americans, or natural forces that emanate around them and in the universe.

If your patients still can't connect to this belief, then have them simply skip this item.

1. It is imperative to empower your patients to love themselves! Self-love is a healthy form of primary narcissism that develops in an infant's interactions with others who fuel love and trust. To love one's self means to care for one's self; self-love does not mean being selfish. Rather, it is a major source of fuel for

establishing a balance between nurturing one's self and caring for others.

2. Recommend that your patients reflect on what they wrote down for self-care on their Fortitude Scale. Have them use that list as a way of exercising love for themselves.

3. Suggest that your patients make a list of all the people they love and have loved in their lifetime. Next to the name of each person, have them write down what it is about that person that they love or have loved so much. Then have them ask, "How can I apply those admirable qualities to myself?"

4. Encourage your patients to tell at least one person a day that they love them. If this is too much, then have them try to do so once a week.

5. Urge your patients to show compassion for others. Help them to help others in need; especially those who are suffering from chronic pain. Support them to share with these other people that they are not alone. Make sure your patients avoid judging people as they shouldn't judge themselves.

6. Have your patients read or listen to the lyrics of love songs, poems, essays, and stories about love.

7. Help your patients seek forgiveness. To forgive others or oneself can be quite a challenge. This can be especially hard if any of your patients have been victims of trauma, including experiencing or witnessing physical, sexual or emotional abuse and they have chronic pain. Many have chronic pain and feel guilty for having thought, said, or acted in ways that have only increased their tension, anger, and problems in interpersonal relationships. Most people are willing to forgive once an apology is made. Others cope with conflicts by walking away, avoiding, or holding onto grudges. This can include caretakers, family or friends. Conflict is a part of life.

    It always amazes me how easy it is to talk to most people to ask for forgiveness. But it takes a lot of courage for others to do so, even in marriages or in close relationships with those who have been your patients' caretakers during difficult times. Help your patients try their best to apologize for "losing it" because of their incredible pain. Seeking forgiveness may come especially hard for those patients who have been the victims of abuse and have chronic pain. I would recommend that your patients read *Forgiveness: How to Make Peace with Your Past and Get on with Your Life* by Sidney and Susan Simon. Another book that may help your patients work through their pain, especially if they still feel angry or seek revenge, is *Forgiveness and Reconciliation: Theory and Application* by Everett L. Worthington Jr.

8. Help your patients learn that "pain" is not just their physical pain. Their anger typically camouflages other, deeper feelings of "pain" like their hurts, disappointments or being misunderstood.

9. On a spiritual level, one can ask for forgiveness from G-d or a higher power. In Hebrew, we call this teshuvah. Asking for forgiveness from G-d or a higher power is easier than one thinks. Your patients don't necessarily have to wait to go to church, synagogue, a mosque, or even an AA meeting. Just encourage them to find a safe space, away from others, and talk, even whisper, or just simply think these thoughts. In Hebrew, it is called "hitbodedut." They won't be considered crazy. King David wasn't crazy when he wrote his beautiful psalms. He shared his pain, asked for G-d's forgiveness and thanked G-d for rescuing him from fear and despair.

10. In his book *Authentic Happiness*, Martin Seligman writes that there is a positive relationship between life satisfaction and one's capacity to forgive. He cites a large Stanford University study which concluded that individuals who participated in a six-session, ninety-minute workshop on forgiveness experienced significantly less anger, less stress, greater optimism and better health than a randomly assigned control group.

Spirituality

"Knock, and He'll open the door.
Vanish, and He'll make you shine like the sun.
Fall, and He'll raise you to the heavens.
Become nothing. And He'll turn you into everything."

\- Jalaluddin Rumi

Your patients' faith in G-d or a higher power could be an ardent healer for their chronic pain.

In his book *On Spirituality,* Abraham Twerski notes that other factors like expressing gratitude (for Twerski, it is "barochot" or blessings in Hebrew) and doing acts of kindness ("chesed" in Hebrew) are empowering factors to enhance one's spirituality. Twerski goes even further to write that one should always celebrate life's positive experiences ("simchahs" in Hebrew), even for those more challenged than others, for it is not for us, as mortal humans, to judge the reasons for which we are given certain medical conditions.

Since I completed my first book, *How to Reduce Your Chronic Pain: A New Model to Restore Your Hope* (2018), I have concluded that having faith can bring much hope for people with chronic pain and their caretakers. This is even true for you, a member of the medical community, who may stress over wanting to help your patients, but realize there is not one single medication or treatment that can eliminate their chronic pain.

In my book, I shared my perspective about how people started to go astray from their faith in G-d in the 1960s. A major theme I presented was that many people's strong faith in G-d, and those in authority, was shattered, first, by the traumatic assassination of President John F. Kennedy in November 1963, then by subsequent historical events, including the Vietnam War, the assassinations of Martin Luther King and Robert F. Kennedy, Watergate and President Nixon, then the Catholic Church sex abuse scandals. In the present day, we have individuals with severe physical and emotional pain from earlier physical and sexual abuse trauma, from alienation, desensitization and dehumanization by advancing technology, and from an inability to "keep up" or utilize multiple fortitude strategies, and we have a national substance and "passive suicide" crisis. This includes the extensive use of opiates, alcohol, antidepressants (the number one substance of reported suicides, followed by alcohol, for 18 states, as noted in *JAMA*, March 2018), and nicotine. As well, the levels of obesity, diabetes, cardiovascular diseases, and people with chronic pain, are at an all-time high, each of which is a comparable crisis to opiates.

I further shared that, due to the rise in substance use disorders, many people have turned to Alcoholics Anonymous (AA) or Narcotics Anonymous

(NA), where, according to a professor-researcher at New York University I heard speak at a Harvard Medical School Conference, the yearning for "spirituality" or belief in a "higher power" is the main reason individuals turn to these specific groups. What the researcher didn't emphasize was that the founder of AA, Bill Wilson, never drank alcohol again following a fourth hospital readmission; this time, to the Towns Hospital in 1934. It was during this hospitalization that, according to Wikipedia, *"while lying in bed depressed and despairing, he cried out, 'I'll do anything! Anything at all! If there be a God, let Him show Himself!' He then had the sensation of a bright light, a feeling of ecstasy, and a new serenity. He never drank again for the remainder of his life. Wilson described his experience to Dr. Silkworth, who told him, 'Something has happened to you I don't understand. But you had better hang on to it."* Apparently, Wilson's commitment was similar to that of his paternal grandfather, who completely stopped drinking after having a similar spiritual experience. Painfully, Wilson had suffered previously through intermittent periods of severe depression, perhaps attributed, to some degree, to a genetic predisposition to alcoholism, to depression, and to his parents abandoning him and his sister after she was born. Bill and his sister were eventually raised by their maternal grandparents.

As difficult as this may sound, your patients' chronic pain is a test of their faith in a manner similar to Bill Wilson, or to the biblical character Job, who lost everything, but regained it all and more when, at the deepest levels of helplessness, hopelessness and despair, he sustained his faith in G-d. As much as your patients wish to have ultimate control of their lives, they can never do so for they are not the Pilot of their journey. Rather, if they can act like Bill Wilson, Job, or even King David, sustaining their faith despite experiencing much suffering and pain, miracles can occur.

Post-Traumatic Stress Disorder, Shame, and Your Patients' Chronic Pain

If your patient had trauma in their life, and currently has chronic pain, then they are not alone! The number of patients I have seen who have had a history of physical or sexual abuse, even in their childhood years, is astonishing. I'm clear there's a high correlation between PTSD and chronic pain.

Remember that "chronic" is reframed as "ongoing, intermittent" and that "pain" is construed as not just being physical. Pain can emanate from life stress, intense emotions of anxiety, depression or anger; from a lack of happiness; from negative thinking; and/or from a lack of fortitude, ranging from simple coping or a lack of self-care, to an inability to be grateful, to love, or to have faith in G-d! Often, one's experience of G-d can be symbolized as one's abusive or neglectful parent or significant other, especially when younger.

Help your patients become aware of what they are holding onto. If they are not using the best ways to deal with their pain, then help them choose to change.

Your patients need to grieve and mourn what they wanted, and what they had! Have them get help for this process, since working through their PTSD pain can become intense. Perceive this therapeutic experience as being no different than the incredible capabilities of your patient's mind and body to increase their temperature or white blood cell count to fight infections.

Once your patients work through the pain of letting go of these conditions associated with PTSD, then they can turn to forgiveness of those who hurt them. Then they can mend and heal.

Your patients' long-term gains emanate from their short-term "pains."

Watch! Their true perception of G-d will become distinguished from "god," the symbol of their abusive or neglectful parent or significant other!

At the end of each Saturday at some Orthodox synagogues, you can hear the service conclude with this verse:

"Do not fear sudden terror, nor the destruction of the wicked when it comes (Proverbs 3:23). Contrive a scheme, but it will be foiled; conspire a plot, but it will not materialize, for G-d is with you (Isaiah 2:10). To your old age, I am with you; I have made you and I will carry you. I will sustain you and deliver you." (Ibid. 46.4)."

There is much comfort in this verse. The hope is that your patients should find comfort in any statements, or acts of faith, especially if they experience chronic pain. They are the navigators of their life jets! As the navigators, who can regulate all the dials (chronic pain rating scales), they must inevitably have ultimate faith that, no matter how much unexpected turbulence they experience, the Pilot will see them through it. Their faith in the Pilot is based on how much total control they believe they have in their lives; consequently, their ratings on spirituality are related to their control scale ratings. There will be times when they feel helpless and powerless. If they can accept helplessness as part of the human condition, then they can have a high spirituality rating.

Recommend that your patients read any books, short stories, quotations, poems, essays, or speeches that enhance their spirituality ratings. Listening to soothing spiritual music can be helpful, as well.

Have your patients set aside some time each day as "sacred time," a term coined by Emile Durkheim. This could be attendance at a religious service, some spiritual period of study, or simply a retreat that allows them to find a space away from stress, even for an hour, where they can meditate, reflect on aspects of their lives that bring them meaningfulness, or simply de-stress.

Encourage your patients to do something nice for somebody else! Doing good deeds and sharing acts of kindness will make them feel good and bring them meaning.

Recommend your patients read and memorize any specific spiritual verses that bring them reassurance that they are not alone. For some of your patients, these may be the sayings of Hillel, the psalms of King David, or Rabbi Nachman of Breslov. For others, it may be the teachings of Jesus, Mohammed, Confucius or Buddha. Encourage your patients to choose those verses that bring them comfort.

Hillel, Ethics of the Fathers, 1:14: *"If I am only for myself, who am I? If not now, when?"*

Psalm 130: *"Grant complete healing to all my wounds, for You, Almighty G-d, are a faithful and merciful healer."*

Psalm 95: *"When I thought that my foot was slipping, Your kindness, O Lord, supported me. When my worrisome thoughts multiply within me, Your consolation delights my soul."*

Psalm 86: *" Your kindness to me has been great; You have saved my soul from the depths of despair."*

Psalm 25: *"Turn to me and be gracious to me, for I am alone and afflicted. The sufferings of my heart have increased; deliver me from my tribulations. Guard my soul and deliver me."*

Isaiah: *" Answer me, O Lord, answer me for I am in great distress. Be near to my cry; let Your loving kindness console me."*

Psalm 147: *"He heals the broken hearted and binds their wounds."*

Psalm 31: *"Just knowing You are listening will quickly rescue me. For You are my boulder and fortress. Take me from this hidden snare, for You are my strength. The snare is the web of worry that my mind hides within me. It appears when I find myself trapped by doubt and fear. Hear my voice clearly saying, "You are my stronghold!" You see my suffering. You know the troubles of my soul. True joy comes from deep within my heart. For when I give myself over to You, I can actualize a sense of real exaltation."*

Psalm 33: *"May You be the source of inner strength and courage to all who long for You. We need not fret the darkness of our night. Instead, we cry out to You. That will give us courage."*

Psalm 25: *"Our hearts become free of dread. No other person can see the extent of my personal suffering for it is unique to my own mind. Only You know what nibbles away at my soul. Have compassion on me, for I am in distress."*

Psalm 23: *"The Lord is my shepherd. I shall lack nothing. He makes me lie down in green pastures. He leads me beside still waters. He restoreth my soul."*

Rabbi Nachman of Breslov: *"If you won't be better tomorrow than you were today, then what do you need tomorrow for?"*

"Grant me the ability to be alone. May it be my custom to go outdoors each day among the trees and grasses among all growing things and there may I be alone, and enter into prayer to talk with the one that I belong to."

"Get into the habit of singing a tune. It will give you new life and fill you with joy. Get into the habit of (imagining yourself) dancing. It will displace depression and dispel hardship."

"Always wear a smile. The gift of life will then be yours to give."

"While praying (Meditating), listen to the words very carefully. When your heart is attentive, your entire being enters your prayer (Meditation) without your having to force it."

"Find a day for yourself -- better yet, late at night. Go to the forest or to the field, or lock yourself in a room ... You will meet solitude there. There you will be able to listen attentively to the noise of the wind first, to birds singing, to see wonderful nature and to notice yourself in it ... and to come back to harmonic connection with the world and its Creator."

"Just as your hand, held before the eye, can hide the tallest mountain, so this small earthly life keeps us from seeing the vast radiance that fills the core of the universe."

"Even if you can't sing well, sing. Sing to yourself. Sing in the privacy of your home. But sing."

"The whole world is a very narrow bridge. And the most important thing is not to be afraid."

"Prayers (Meditations) truly from the heart open all doors in Heaven."

"Let us acquire a heart of wisdom to understand the design of our body, the proportions of its joints and the structure of its limbs. This necessary understanding helps us to know the Creator Who formed all these creations. Who heals all sickness and each one's pains -- the blind and the lame, the leprous and afflicted, he who worries and he who is in pain. Let us eat only to sustain our souls, restraining our natural cravings. Chazak! Be strong!"

Luke 6:8, *"Do to others as you would have them do to you."*

John 4:7, *"Let us love one another, for love comes from G-d. Everyone who loves has been born of G-d and knows G-d."*

John 4:8, *"Whoever does not love does not know G-d, because G-d is love."*

Prophet Mohammad: *"Those who love will be loved by the Most Loving. So love those on Earth and those in Heaven will love you."*

Quran 25:63: *"The servants of the most loving are those who walk on the earth in humility, and when the ignorant address them, they say, 'Peace!' "*

Quran 49:13: *"In G-d's eyes the most noble of you are those who are the most mindful of Him: G-d is all knowing, all aware."*

Confucius: *"Wheresoever you go, go with all your heart!"*
"What you do not want done to yourself, do not do to others."
"Wherever you go, there you are."

Buddha: *"You can search throughout the entire universe for someone who is more deserving of your love and affection than you are yourself, and that person is not to be found anywhere. You, yourself, as much as anybody in the entire universe, deserve your love and affection."*

"When you realize how perfect everything is you will tilt your head back and laugh at the sky."

"I understand with love comes pain, but why did I have to love so much?"

Take a bow for a pain-free life!

Chapter 13: Conclusion

It should be clear by now that no one is free of pain, even from an early age. Don't let anyone tell you differently. Pain is a metaphor. It's not just your patients' physical pain. If we thought that our opiate addiction crisis is bad, a recent study indicated a 36% increase in alcohol use disorders between 2012 and 2013. The largest increase is for patients over age 65. Even cocaine use is on the rise as is the risk of death for individuals who combine antidepressants with alcohol. As mentioned earlier, your patients are experiencing intense pain from experiences like obesity, diabetes, high cholesterol, lack of exercise, life stress, anxiety, depression, trauma, boredom, phone and other technology addictions, the need for immediate gratification, and an inability to have strong fortitude skills. We have a significant "passive suicide" crisis going on, comparable to the Black Death plague of the Middle Ages!

How can you help to reduce your patients' chronic pain?

As a healthcare provider, perceive your role as a challenge, as an opportunity, rather than an experience of frustration, stress and sometimes, despair. You have the ability to help your patients fight it and this book's model of a Pain Management Lifestyle gives you the tools to fight and triumph.

Acknowledgements

I wish to thank Aaron Beck and Martin Seligman for helping to transform our way of thinking and improving our patients' health and happiness.

I wish to thank Kate Victory Hannisian of Blue Pencil Consulting for her diligence in editing and proofreading this book, and Brian Murphy of Brian Murphy Art and Design for his creative gift in graphic art and design.

I want to thank Drs. Gilmore O'Neal, Terrance Doorly, Leon Jenis, and Jacob Freedman for giving me hope through quite a medical ordeal of having six surgeries in seven years.

I want to thank all the specialists who helped me along the way on my own path towards living a Pain Management Lifestyle.

Finally, I want to thank G-d for giving me a second chance! And the opportunity to help those 100 million people who suffer from chronic pain to turn back to Him.

About the Author

George Beilin, EdD, is a seasoned, licensed psychologist with over 46 years of clinical experience and has specialized in the treatment of patients who have chronic pain. He obtained his master's degree in 1972 and his doctorate in psychology in 1976 from Boston University. Dr. Beilin was the chief psychologist for the pain center at Lahey Outpatient Center at Danvers, Massachusetts, where he evaluated and treated multiple patients for various pain disorders. He has facilitated a free, weekly chronic pain support group.

Dr. Beilin formulated his theoretical model for reducing chronic pain from his interest in the trans-theoretical model of change and a bio-psycho-social approach to perceiving pain as being influenced by multiple sources other than simply physical ones. He emphasizes building fortitude and reframing chronic pain as a challenge rather than an obstruction in one's life. His empathy for patients with chronic pain stems from enduring his own chronic pain from six major surgeries in seven years.

Dr. Beilin has been married for over 40 years to his wife, Stephanie, a Licensed Psychiatric Social Worker who is employed by the Danvers Public Schools. They reside in Hamilton, Massachusetts.